THE GOD OF SECOND CHANCES

The God of Second Chances

Finding Hope through the Prophets of Exile

RON CLARK

CASCADE *Books* • Eugene, Oregon

THE GOD OF SECOND CHANCES
Finding Hope through the Prophets of Exile

Copyright © 2012 Ron Clark. All rights reserved. Except for brief quotations in critical publications or reviews, no part of this book may be reproduced in any manner without prior written permission from the publisher. Write: Permissions, Wipf and Stock Publishers, 199 W. 8th Ave., Suite 3, Eugene, OR 97401.

Cascade Books
An Imprint of Wipf and Stock Publishers
199 W. 8th Ave., Suite 3
Eugene, OR 97401

www.wipfandstock.com

ISBN 13: 978-1-62032-083-9

Cataloging-in-Publication data:

Clark, Ron

    The god of second chances : finding hope through the prophets of exile / Ron Clark.

    viii + 180 p.; 23 cm—Includes bibliographical references.

    ISBN 13: 978-1-62032-083-9

    1. Bible—O. T.—Prophets—Criticism, interpretation, etc. 2. Jews—History—Babylonian captivity (598–515 B.C.). 3. Abused women—Pastoral counseling of. 4. Abusive men—Pastoral counseling of.

BV4445.5 C56 2012

Unless otherwise noted, all Scripture quotations are the author's own translations. Scriptures marked (NRSV) are taken from New Revised Standard Version Bible, copyright © 1989, Division of Christian Education of the National Council of the Churches of Christ in the United States of America. Used by permission. All rights reserved.

Manufactured in the USA

Contents

Acknowledgments | *vii*

PART ONE	Introduction: The God of Hope
1	Meeting the God of Second Chances	3
2	How Did We Get Here?	18
3	Who Were the Prophets?	37

PART TWO	Advocates for Hope
4	Jeremiah: God in Therapy, Working with Both for Reconciliation	49
5	Obadiah: Compassion and Empathy in God's House	69
6	Habakkuk: Crying Out for Mercy	77
7	Zephaniah: Voices in the Heart of the City	88

PART THREE	Visionaries of Hope
8	Joel: Offering Hope during the Storm	99
9	Ezekiel: Sharing Anger, Sharing Exile, Sharing Hope	109
10	Haggai: Replacing Shame with Hope in a New Life	124
11	Zechariah: Continual Reminders That Develop Hope	137

Contents

PART FOUR   Calling for Hope
    12   Malachi: Confronting Those Who Destroy Hope | 151
    13   Jesus, the God of Second Chances | 165

    Bibliography | 177

Acknowledgments

This book is the first in a series of three for ministers, Christians, and the missional-incarnational church. I began a series on the prophets at the Agape Church of Christ in 2010 and will continue with Luke and Acts. My hope is that Christians will be energized by both the text and our ministry—not only to reflect God's glory but to live the vision Jesus has for all people.

My family has been such a great support for me in this work. Lori has been my partner in ministry and our work in the community for almost twenty-five years. Thank you for being with me in this journey and mentoring so many people in the faith. Nathan, you have grown to be a great man of God, and I know that you will carry this passion to whatever you do after college. Hunter and Caleb, thanks for helping me unwind after a hard day at work and keeping me focused on what really matters to kids—having a dad who is in your life.

The Agape Church of Christ has been such a great blessing to us as well. You have journeyed through the biblical text with us and given us a place to test the theology of Jesus. So many of the stories in this book came from you, and it is a joy to read them and see so many of you who have changed your lives through the power of Jesus. It has been a joy to preach to you and watch you train others to start new churches.

Dr. Mark Hamilton of Abilene Christian University, Dr. David Fleer of Lipscomb University, Dr. Len Sweet of George Fox Evangelical Seminary, Dr. Walter Brueggemann of Columbia Theological Seminary, Marshall Snyder and Kevin Palau of Portland were very helpful in reading through this work and offering feedback. As always K. C. Hanson,

Acknowledgments

James Stock, and Christian Amondson have been a great help in support to publish my work and make it available for others to read.

Ron Clark
Agape Church of Christ
www.agapecoc.com

PART ONE

Introduction: The God of Hope

1

Meeting the God of Second Chances

One rainy Portland morning I was riding the light rail, called the MAX, downtown. A couple times a week I would take the MAX to be among people and see who God put in my path. We were planting a new church in this city and developing a newer style of ministry. Usually I would take whoever I met living on the streets, homeless, or asking for money, and would buy them lunch. This was always a growing experience for me because I learned to listen to their stories and opinions about life, God, and Portland. I realized that most of us, as Laura Stivers suggests, are only one paycheck away from being in their shoes.[1] I also found that I developed friendships with many of them and would learn their names, desires, and dreams, especially when they would visit Agape.

As I stepped off the MAX I realized that it was too cold, too wet, and too late in the morning. I felt led to walk toward the bridges, but would mumble to myself and God, "No, its too late, no one will be here . . ." Directly following God's leading in how I used my time felt awkward because I had previously spent over twenty years in established churches with organized schedules and regular office hours. People came to see me when they wanted help. The Spirit, I felt, was more a rational and logical force that guided us morally to be like God. It took only two months of planting this new church to realize that the Spirit led or drove people

---

1. Stivers, *Disrupting Homelessness*, 2.

PART ONE   Introduction: The God of Hope

to where God was already working. In this case I felt compelled to go under the Portland bridges to find someone God was trying to help. Even though I mumbled and argued with God, it seemed that I still kept walking along the waterfront, looking for people still huddled by one of the pillars of a bridge, hoping to stay warm. People who heard me talking may have thought I was one of the wandering residents who had forgotten to take their medication.

This morning I saw no one under the first two bridges. "See," I sighed, "no people—too cold, too wet, too late—just like I said." I kept walking up a slight grassy hill, cutting across the waterfront park toward the next bridge, known as the Steel Bridge. In the light rain and fog I could see my breath in the air. I began to walk faster and faster. "I'll get back on the MAX and go to Pioneer Square," I mumbled; "there will be plenty of people there. If not, I will hang out at Starbucks and read or pray." I began to see the giant Steel Bridge in the fog as I exhaled; my warm breath covered what little bit I could see of the bridge. As I moved closer to the bridge, I saw a red jacket in a gap by the bridge supports. "OK, this isn't funny, God," I said. Another five steps and I realized that it was a young man—eighteen or nineteen years old—wearing a red jacket. He was sitting on the ground, huddled under his coat, and shivering.

"Hey, are you OK?" I asked. He just looked at me and put his head back down.

"You cold?" I said.

He nodded his head yes.

"Hey, man, let's go get something warm to eat. I'll buy. I think you could probably use some coffee and a hot meal. What do you say?"

He looked straight in my eyes, slowly shrugged his shoulders, and got up. I asked him his name, and he acted as if he didn't want to talk.

"Mark" he finally said.

We headed toward a Chinese restaurant I knew that served hot tea, dim sung, and a variety of cheap food. Mark was a tall, skinny, and tired-looking kid.

After he began to eat and drink, he started talking about where he was from. "Why you doing this, man?" he whined. "Why you doing this to me?"

It was a good question. Portland has been known as Boys Town because of the many pedophiles who hang around the downtown and seek sex from the street boys in exchange for booze, drugs, or a place to stay. I hadn't thought about it much but could see why he was nervous.

Meeting the God of Second Chances

"Mark, I don't want anything from you. I am buying you lunch, and when you're done you can leave, no strings attached," I said.

He ate and stayed awhile. We talked about his life: his controlling mother, her shoving religion down his throat, his fear of never pleasing his parents, and his drug addiction. Mark had been through treatment twice and had turned back to heroin, his drug of choice. Now he was nineteen, homeless, and sleeping under a bridge. In his coat pocket was a tallboy can of beer and he was planning to drink it for lunch. Again he asked, "I just can't believe you're taking me out to lunch for no reason. I know you said you are a Christian, but that's just not what I'm used to seeing with Christians. Why you doing this, man?"

"I don't know," I said, "I guess I'm just a man with a second chance in ministry to finally start practicing unconditional love for people. I am doing this because God has shown me that my past twenty years of ministry were too focused on the wrong people."

"Well," he mumbled, "forgiveness is not something I'm used to, and I grew up going to church. I know God did all that stuff in the Bible and punished people for bad things, but I don't see that love and forgiveness people always talk about. I don't even see it in other church people. It's hard for me to believe in a forgiving and loving God."

We had a great lunch, and I hugged Mark, prayed with him, and told him I loved him. I also said that God loved him more than I ever could, and that I would be praying for him.

"I know," he said, "I'll remember this." Then he was gone.

The sun was breaking through the typical Portland fog, the bridges were in sight, and I had learned more during this meal than I had learned in any theology class. How could someone grow up in church and not know that God was passionate about loving people? How could a parent harass and control a child with a faith that is based on free will? Is love controlling or is love empowering?

How Did We Miss This?

"The days are coming," declares Yahweh, "when they will no longer say, 'As Yahweh lives, who brought the Israelites up out of Egypt,' they will say, 'As Yahweh lives, who brought the Israelites from the north and out of all the countries where they were banished.' I will restore them to the land I gave their forefathers" (Jer 16:14–15).[2]

For most of my life I understood that the Passover/exodus was one of the greatest events in Israelite history. From my early days in Sunday school, and later years in church, I heard how God led the Israelites (and a few Egyptian people) out of Egypt to freedom. The story of Moses, the plagues, and the hardhearted pharaoh was told every year by my teachers and shown through television movies. The story of the Passover lamb being slaughtered was shared during Easter. I knew that the Jewish people celebrated this Passover as one of the greatest and most memorable events in their history. Even Christians would discuss Jesus's last meal, the Lord's Supper, and his death on the cross as a reflection of the Passover. We were taught that Jesus was the Passover lamb and that communion also had origins in this Jewish festival. I even knew that Jewish Christians would celebrate the Passover Seder before Easter and encouraged Gentile Christians to eat with them.

The Judean kings Hezekiah and Josiah restored the Passover celebration to their people (2 Chronicles 30 and 35). The kings before them had not only drifted away from serving Yahweh, but they had abandoned this holy festival. God's people were commanded to keep this celebration every year and suffered for allowing it to lapse. Hezekiah and Josiah reinstated this great event, which brought God's blessings on their people. The return of this event also attracted those outside Jerusalem and became a festival of grace, acceptance, and forgiveness. The Passover was truly one of the greatest festivals for the Judean people.

This festival was a reminder that God had heard the cries of the oppressed Israelites while they were suffering under their Egyptian tormentor and king, Pharaoh (Exod 3:7–10). God had sent ten plagues upon the Egyptians, which eventually led to the Israelites' expulsion from the land. The final plague was the death of every firstborn male, which even included the child of Pharaoh. In order to avert this plague, the Israelites (and those Egyptians who listened to Moses) butchered a lamb and smeared the blood on their doorposts. The annual Passover celebration involved a meal with lamb and with vegetables, and the story of God's delivering the Hebrew people from bondage. This festival was a celebration of God's power and love, and of the beginnings of a new relationship.

---

2. Unless otherwise noted, Bible quotations are my translations of the Hebrew and Greek texts.

Yet, according to the Jeremiah passage quoted above, one event would become more prominent than the Passover. It would be an event that would symbolize a new perspective on Yahweh that may not have been understood by Jeremiah's contemporaries.

The kingdom of Israel was torn into two kingdoms shortly after the death of King Solomon, who was also known as the wisest king. While Solomon was historically a wise king, his greed for money, women, and power oppressed the people of Israel. One of Solomon's commanders, Jeroboam, took ten of the twelve tribes and formed the northern kingdom, also called *Israel*, and built his headquarters at the city of *Shechem*. Solomon's son, Rehoboam, kept the two remaining tribes (Judah and Benjamin), as well as the tribe of priests known as the Levites, and remained in *Jerusalem*. This was called the southern kingdom or *Judah*. The northern kingdom continued to rebel against Yahweh by worshiping idols and practicing injustice. In the middle of the eighth century BCE, the world power, Assyria, attacked the city of Samaria (which had become the capital of Israel, the northern kingdom), captured the people, and transported them to Nineveh (2 Kgs 17:1–6). Samaria was repopulated with foreign people who brought their religions and lifestyles to the city's squatters. Israel had lost their home, identity, and lineage.

The southern kingdom, however, was ruled by some kings who obeyed Yahweh and by others who rebelled against God. At the beginning of the sixth century BCE God allowed the new world power's king, Nebuchadnezzar of Babylon, to destroy the city of Jerusalem. "Who handed Jacob over to become loot, and Israel to the plunderers? Was it not Yahweh, against whom we have sinned? For they would not follow God's ways; they did not obey the law" (Isa 42:24). The city was attacked three times in ten years, and the elite citizens were transported to Babylon. A handful of people were left behind to survive in the ruins of the city. Jeremiah the prophet told the captives in Babylon, that they were to settle in the city, build houses, work for the government, and bless their city for seventy years (Jer 29:7). Jeremiah also encouraged them, and shared that God would bring the next generation home to Jerusalem in seventy years: "This is what Yahweh Almighty, the God of Israel, says to those I carried into exile from Jerusalem to Babylon: 'Build houses and settle down; plant gardens and eat what they produce. Marry and have sons and daughters; find wives for your sons and give your daughters in marriage, so that they too may have sons and daughters. Increase in number there; do not decrease. Seek the peace and prosperity of the city

PART ONE   Introduction: The God of Hope

to which I have carried you into exile. Pray to Yahweh for it, because if it prospers, you will as well'" (Jer 29:4–7).

The passage above suggests that Yahweh would again lead the people back to Jerusalem, as God had done in the exodus from Egypt.[3] This second exodus, however, exhibited God's forgiveness. Yahweh not only led the Israelites out of Egypt, but God brought the people home from captivity. Yahweh would be the hero who brought them home, gave them a second chance, and restored their kingdom.

In the story of the Passover, Yahweh was the one who freed the Israelites from slavery. In the return from exile Yahweh would be the one who forgave, who reconciled, and who restored their relationship. Those separated from their God would be united once again: "Surely Yahweh's arm is not too short to save, nor ear too dull to hear. Your disobedience has separated you from your God; your sins have hidden you from God's presence, so that they are not heard" (Isa 59:1–2).

However, the exile was different. While the people of God may have been exploited, oppressed, and abused in Babylon, this captivity happened because they chose to abandon their God. The exile occurred because their leaders had failed to obey their Lord. They courted the favor and support of other powerful kingdoms while refusing to trust Yahweh for their protection and care. Yet God again desired to lead them out of this slavery, captivity, and oppression. However, this time it would manifest itself as power through forgiveness, mercy, and hope of a new relationship. God's strength would be displayed through rebuilding lives, pouring out the Spirit of healing and forgiveness, establishing another covenant/relationship, and restoring Judean life and identity. Even though the Jerusalem temple had been destroyed, God still lived among the people through the Spirit and leaders such as Ezekiel, Jeremiah, Daniel, Esther, Ezra, Nehemiah, and others. Yahweh would prove to be the God of second, third, fourth, and multiple chances.

It seems that this great historical event of exile and deliverance is absent from our church history. Have we missed these stories? Have we not seen the greater event in Judean history? Has Christian understanding of biblical history ended with the exodus and revived at Matthew? I find that many Christians misunderstand the prophets and the stories of captivity, as well as the restoration of Jerusalem. This misunderstanding in turn affects our conception of Jesus's ministry and the ministry

---

3. "It is undeniable that the return from exile was seen as a fulfillment of the expectation of the second exodus" (Longman, *How to Read Exodus*, 150).

Meeting the God of Second Chances

of the church. We struggle to understand the restoration of Judah for two reasons.

One reason may be that we *misapply* the Hebrew Scriptures (commonly labeled the Old Testament). Many times we Christians exploit the prophets by reading their words only as predictions of Jesus. We carefully mine the texts, looking for announcements of the Messiah and reinterpret these passages only in light of Jesus. The prophets then become a springboard to the Christian Scriptures (also known as the New Testament). Most Christians have studied very little of the prophets in their original context and only use them to hurry through the Old Testament in order to read Matthew's gospel. Then, we believe, it will all begin to make sense. Jesus, we are told, fulfills the prophets, making all prophecies come true in this present time and age. If this is true, then the prophets had little meaning to or hope for their original audiences. Imagine the people suffering while their prophets told them that in a few hundred years the Messiah would come to help other generations to freedom. What hope would this provide the hearers?

Another reason we struggle to understand the restoration involves our terminology for Bible sections. We use the term "Old Testament" for the Bible books from Genesis to Malachi, and "New Testament" for the books from Matthew to Revelation. This is our traditional terminology, but it is wrong. *Testament* means "covenant." The old testament or covenant refers to a broken covenant violated by God's people which ended (Exod 32:1–20; Heb 9:1–5; Jer 31:32). The new testament/covenant, therefore, refers to a renewed or reestablished covenant relationship between God and the people (Jer 31:31; Luke 22:20; Heb 8:8). Israel violated, or broke faith with, God and the covenant. This happened when the people worshiped the gold calf (Exodus 32), when they as a people clung to other gods (2 Kgs 17:36–41), and as the people embraced a foreign culture. When Israel broke these covenants, they were punished. However, Yahweh initiated relationship again by establishing a new covenant and reconciling with the people as they returned home (Exodus 35; Jeremiah 31–34).

In Jesus, Yahweh initiated another covenant as well (Luke 22:20; Heb 8:3). The Hebrew term for "new" also meant "renewed." When the writer of the book labeled Hebrews described the old or first covenant as having no effect on the Christian, some readers may assume that the writer is calling ineffectual what we today call the Old Testament or Hebrew Scriptures (see Heb 8:13—"By saying that this [covenant] is new/renewed [God] makes the first one old and that which is becoming old and

PART ONE Introduction: The God of Hope

worn out will soon disappear"). However, this is inaccurate. In the book of Hebrews, the "old covenant" refers to the broken covenants of the past. Since we have typically understood the term "Old Testament" to refer to certain books of our Bible, many Christians might assume that this part of our Bible has little, if any, use for us today. We should use language that combines all these books into one living text useful for all people. The term "Bible" or the terms "Hebrew Scriptures" and "Christian Scriptures" seem to capture all texts and themes together. The Bible is a continuous story of God's work with creation. This continuous story helps us to understand Israelite history and the role of the captivity and restoration of Jerusalem in the development of God's relationship with people.

Because we Christians often miss these wonderful stories of God, we are unable to see Yahweh and Jesus fully in the gospels and early Christian writings. Jesus's fulfillment of prophetic passages suggests that Jesus came to complete them, again. The Gospel of Luke's terminology of restoration, comfort, and consolation suggests that the early Christian communities were to be groups of people restored and reconciled to Yahweh through the Spirit. The pouring out and baptism of the Spirit was a sign that God was reestablishing a relationship with all people through Jesus (Matt 3:11–12; Luke 3:16; Acts 2:1–28). The contemporary Christian church likewise is to be a place where people heal and receive or revive a relationship with the God of second, third, fourth, and more chances. The Christian church, like the exiles returning from captivity, are to be a people reconciled to God. through Jesus. The church represents an empire or kingdom of people restored to harmony with God and others: "Some asked [Jesus], 'Lord, are you at this time going to restore/reestablish the kingdom to Israel?' He said to them: 'It is not for you to know the periods or times set by the Father's own authority. But you will receive power when the Holy Spirit comes on you; and you will be my witnesses in Jerusalem, all Judea, Samaria, and the end of the earth'" (Acts 1:6–8).

This emphasis on restored relationships seems even clearer when we read Jesus's call to Peter in Luke 5. When Jesus caused the fishermen's nets to fill, Peter realized Jesus's power: "Seeing this, Simon Peter fell by Jesus's knees and said, 'Go away from me, Lord; I am a sinful man!' He and all those with him were amazed at the catch of fish they had; so were James and John, the sons of Zebedee, Simon's partners. Then Jesus said to Simon, 'Don't be afraid; from now on you will catch people.' They pulled their boats up on shore, left everything and followed him" (Luke 5:8–11).

Jesus's call for Peter to "catch" people is very similar to Jeremiah's encouragement that the returned exiles "catch" people for God (Jer 16:14–16). Peter was invited not only to preach for Jesus, but to be a key component in the gathering of the spiritual exiles in first-century Israel.

God in the Prophets

In reading the prophets, we not only understand that the return of the exiles was to be a major event in Israelite history. We also come to understand that Yahweh's nature was revealed further through these exilic prophets. *First, God will not be abused and victimized in a relationship.* The captivity was a sign that the kingdoms of Israel and Judah had been divorced by their God. Because they had violated God's covenant and abused their "father" and "husband," Yahweh took an aggressive stance by "divorcing" them or sending them away:

> I gave faithless Israel her certificate of divorce and sent her away because of all her adulteries. Yet I saw that her unfaithful sister Judah had no fear; she also went out and committed adultery. (Jer 3:8)

> "Yahweh will call you back as if you were a wife deserted and distressed in spirit—a wife who married young, only to be rejected," says your God. (Isa 54:6)

> This is what Yahweh says: "Where is your mother's certificate of divorce with which I sent her away? Or to which of my creditors did I sell you? Because of your sins you were sold; because of your disobedience your mother was sent away. (Isa 50:1)

> I took my staff called Favor and cut it in half, to violate the covenant I had made with all the nations." (Zech 11:10)

This metaphor of divorce was a sign that God had abandoned the people. The biblical texts are clear that Yahweh had taken enough of the people's sinful and dysfunctional behavior. The Israelites believed that God would not abandon them (Deut 31:6, 8; Josh 1:9). However, the biblical texts tell us that God has the right and the option to end a relationship with someone who violates the covenant or agreement. "To modern audiences the God of the marriage metaphor may be much too violent to endure. But to Israel it was a portrait that was too honest and

PART ONE   Introduction: The God of Hope

consistent with reality as they knew it to deny."[4] Yahweh is called "faithful" in Hebrew, which suggests that God does not violate the covenant. However, the people of Israel had repeatedly turned their backs on God, worshiped other deities, oppressed the poor and vulnerable, and turned from following Yahweh: "It is no wonder that God's and Zion's voices cannot organically inhabit the same text. What the text reveals, counter intuitively for many of us, is that God's love does have limits. This may seem reasonable, especially in human terms—why should anyone love those who are not loyal to them? This is not a groundbreaking discovery, but it is instructive to delineate how the text actually lays this out, naturalizes it, and thereby hides it in plain view."[5]

Since Israel had broken their covenant and broken faith, God was not obliged to maintain the relationship. Handed over to their enemies, they were abandoned by their Lord: "The reason why Yahweh has decided to abandon his people is that they have already abandoned him. Looking over the social landscape, the prophetic eye discovers a scene of massive God-neglect. The people do not include Yahweh meaningfully in the practical reality of their lives, where real faith is tested. Instead, they have staked their lives on the Baals, discarding the reality of God and embracing the unreality of counterfeit gods."[6]

This is even more clearly displayed in how Yahweh dealt with Israel during the destruction of their capital cities (Samaria and Jerusalem). As their enemies leveled their cities, the suffering people prayed to Yahweh. However, God ignored their cries and commanded the prophets to do the same:

> Although they cry out to me, I will not listen to them. The towns of Judah and the people of Jerusalem will go and cry out to the gods to whom they burn incense, but they will not help them at all when disaster strikes. Do not pray for this people or offer any plea or petition for them, because I will not listen when they call to me in the time of their distress. (Jer 11:11–14)

> Then Yahweh said to me, "Do not pray for the well-being of this people. Although they fast, I will not listen to their cry; though they offer burnt offerings and grain offerings, I will not accept them. Instead, I will destroy them with the sword, famine, and plague." (Jer 14:11–12)

---

4. Weems, *Battered Love*, 83.
5. Mandolfo, *Daughter Zion*, 118.
6. Ortlund, *Whoredom*, 97.

> My God will reject them because they have not obeyed/listened; they will be wanderers among the nations/Gentiles. (Hos 9:17)

> For he [King Manessah] had filled Jerusalem with innocent blood, which Yahweh was unwilling to forgive. (2 Kgs 24:4)

God cannot be manipulated. The kingdoms of Israel and Judah thought that Yahweh would be faithful, regardless of their disobedience. However, they were wrong. Even during the last few moments of their lives, they could not expect to call on Yahweh and receive salvation.

Second, in the writings of the prophets, *salvation rests completely in the hands of Yahweh.* The texts above indicate that God has the options either to forgive and save or to not forgive and not save. Too often Christians believe that if they use the correct formula of repentance, confession, and contrition they have guaranteed forgiveness. The Bible cannot be reduced to a mathematical formula. It tells us what God wants, shows us God's nature; but it also tells us that God *chooses* to forgive, *chooses* to love, and *chooses* to save. I cannot force God to save or forgive me based on a prayer, confession, or act of repentance. In fact, God always has the option to say no to me.

Faith is that hope and belief that God can forgive us when we confess our sins and make amends to God and others. Faith fills in the gaps and provides assurance when we doubt. All people, when approaching the throne of God's grace, have doubts and uncertainties concerning God's ability or willingness to forgive their sins. However, faith reminds me that God's nature is compassion, mercy, and love. Faith is not a formula to manipulate our creator into forgiving us and giving us a pass to heaven, faith is shown in courageously approaching the Lord of all and trusting the choices made by our creator. In the end, faith accepts what God chooses to do, knowing that the Lord will do what is right, not by our standards but by God's.

In the book of Daniel the three Judeans Shadrach, Meshach, and Abednego were unwilling to worship the Babylonian king's image. The king threatened to kill them, but they would not submit to his will. The king even proclaimed that their God could not save them. For King Nebuchadnezzar, his god (Marduk) had clearly defeated the Judean God, Yahweh, which was why he thought that these young men were captives in Babylon. That God did not save them in the past (Jer 11:11–14) suggested to Nebuchadnezzar that Yahweh was powerless. It also suggested to the three Judeans that God may or may not save their lives when they

PART ONE   Introduction: The God of Hope

were tested. However, they still obeyed their God: "Shadrach, Meshach and Abednego replied to the king, 'Nebuchadnezzar, we do not need to defend ourselves before you in this matter. If we are thrown into the blazing furnace, the God we serve is able to save and rescue us from your hand, king. But if not, we want you to know, king, that we will not serve your gods or worship the image of gold you have set up'" (Dan 3:16–19). There was a sense of uncertainty in their minds as to whether Yahweh would physically save them. However, they indicated to Nebuchadnezzar that their relationship with God was based on *their belief that Yahweh was their master and deserved complete submission.*

A third observation about God in the prophetic writings is that *it is within Yahweh's nature to forgive, practice mercy, and restore relationships.* Some of the prophets express a description of God that is common in the Hebrew Scriptures. Yahweh is a God of mercy, compassion, forgiveness, and love.

> Yahweh, Yahweh, the compassionate and gracious God, slow to anger, abounding in love and faithfulness, maintaining love to thousands, and forgiving wickedness, rebellion and sin. (Exod 34:6)

> I knew that you are a gracious and compassionate God, slow to anger and abounding in love, a God who changes from sending calamity. (Jonah 4:2)

> Yahweh is good, a safe place in a day of trouble, and one who knows those who seek protection/safety. (Nah 1:7)

> But you Lord are a compassionate and gracious God, slow to anger, abounding in faithfulness/love and trustworthiness. (Ps 86:15)

This is the nature of God and the description commonly ascribed to Yahweh. As we come to God in prayer, we don't demand forgiveness—we ask for it. We appeal to God's nature. We ask God to choose. We confess our struggles as we admit our weakness. The prophets tell us that God makes choices, and we should never assume that we can manipulate the creator of the world. God is just and will choose what is right. The question is, will we accept that decision?

We sometimes expect, demand, or plan on God forgiving us. We also expect others to forgive. Forgiveness is no longer a choice; it is a guarantee—or so we believe. For many victims of abuse forgiveness is forced. The offender does not have to repent, but we are expected to automatically forgive them when they say they are sorry. (In a similar way, many expect God to automatically forgive when they are sorry.) Instead of a choice, forgiveness becomes a trump card. We may believe that if we pray enough or pray the right way, we will get results, because it seems that God has little choice in the matter and that we are the ones controlling repentance, forgiveness, and grace. We have no room in our theology for a God who *may choose not to forgive*. This mystery is something we are uncomfortable accepting.

Often when I teach this point, some Christians become disturbed. People tell me that they always understood we had a guarantee of forgiveness when we prayed. Some suggest that I am causing people to leave the presence of God unsure of forgiveness, salvation, or mercy. Others tell me that if they cannot know they have forgiveness, then they will spend their lives worrying about being good enough. Others even assert that I am preaching a God who cannot help people. This anxiety suggests to me that we have become too comfortable with a formula prayer for forgiveness. We have neglected repentance. For some, repentance is saying, I'm sorry, rather than changing one's life, making amends, or modifying behavior. Christianity has spent much energy making sure that people "know they are saved" and therefore has removed the power and mystery from God. Forgiveness then becomes a responsibility that God has to fulfill in order to make us feel better. We are uncomfortable with approaching God's presence with any mystery or uncertainty because such mystery places great weight on repentance and on our willingness to trust the creator regardless of the outcome. We want answers and we seem to expect them from God. However, the prophets tell us that Yahweh is *God*. In the ancient world, gods did what they pleased. Their people had little say in the matter. Yahweh is different. Yahweh is the one true God, whose nature is to forgive, love, and extend grace. Yet this is God's choice because God is love. When we approach God in prayer, we have assurance that we serve the Lord of mercy; however, there is little we can do to earn that mercy.

Fourth, in the prophets we find that *God's nature is sometimes manifested by not intervening*. In some stories God intervened and healed the sick, protected the weak, and overthrew kingdoms. Yet typically God allows bad things to happen rather than intervene. Yahweh allowed rulers to destroy kingdoms, oppress others, and violate the Torah. God sent prophets to warn the people but let years pass before punishing them. God allowed Israel and Judah to practice wickedness for decades and

PART ONE   Introduction: The God of Hope

even centuries before calling the Assyrians and Babylonians to destroy the cities. The suffering of the Judeans was not directly by the hand of Yahweh, it was by the hands of others.

Finally, the prophets indicate that *God has a strong passion for people.* Yahweh initiated relationships, even with those who rebelled and rejected their creator. Yahweh gave visions of hope, trust, love, and forgiveness to a people too weak to care. Yahweh hoped that the people would see how much their God loved them and return that same love. Yahweh gave to a people who habitually took and failed to reciprocate. Yahweh loved a people as a father and mother love their children and as one spouse loves the other. God used intimate terms for the people of Israel, such words as a young lover might use trying to woo a mate. Yahweh displayed passion by a willingness to trust, hope, dream, and love. This is a God whose forgiveness can be as shocking as Israel's unfaithfulness would have been.[7]

Yahweh's nature is expressed by the prophets. In their writings we encounter God and learn whom we are serving. When the Israelites left Egypt, they traveled into the wilderness and met their God. They learned that Yahweh loved them, was awesome and powerful, did not tolerate being neglected, and could provide for them and protect them from every sickness, army, and disaster. After the Babylonian exile, the Judeans returned home to see that Yahweh was a God who had been victimized and neglected, yet one willing to forgive, a God who wanted a relationship, who dreamed about them, hoped for the best in them, and wanted to bless them. This God whom they met was the same God as in the exodus, but manifested later as a God who the people needed in order to rebuild their lives. Even more, this God pursued a relationship with them. To forgive the one who had the affair would have been incredible for Jewish males, yet to forgive is Yahweh's nature, which gives us assurance to come to God in prayer.

The God of Second Chances

Imagine someone who suspects a spouse of having an affair. Imagine the fear, the anxiety, and the constant pain that would go through the person's mind. Imagine how hard it would be for that one to try to talk to the spouse only to be ignored or told to stop imagining things.

---

7. Weems, *Battered Love*, 32.

Meeting the God of Second Chances

Imagine that this man or woman follows his or her partner to a hotel. He or she waits a half hour and then musters the courage to go to the hotel room and knock on the door. As the door opens, the other spouse stands at the door in a robe. Over the shoulder of this partner, another is seen lying in the bed under the covers. The onlooker at the door sees two wine glasses and clothes strewn across the floor. Then the discovered spouse says, "This means nothing . . ." Or, "Let me explain . . ."; or even worse, "You drove me to this . . ."

"The prophet suspects that the very notion that the husband is willing to take his wife back, to reclaim her after she has become defiled by other men, that he is willing to start anew, and that he will trust her unconditionally again is unimaginable to his male Hebrew audience. Indeed, never could his audience imagine that a husband might take his adulterous wife back so lovingly, so gently, with such trust."[8] Even more remember that we are not the ones in the hotel room. We may be in the passenger seat observing what happened and listening to God. We are observing a conversation between a hurt spouse and a hurtful spouse. We are there to listen to God, support God, grieve with God, and learn from the incident. In the exilic prophets we not only meet the God of second chances, but we grieve with Yahweh and see the heart and passion of one who is relationship and who seeks relationship with the creation.

8. Ibid., 50.

2

How Did We Get Here?

Let death and exile and every other thing which appears dreadful be daily before your eyes . . . —Epictetus, *Enchiridion* XXI

Modern Exiles

DIGNITY VILLAGE IS A transitional community for the homeless in Portland. In 2002 a group of eighty people who lived under various Portland bridges banded together with others from the community and requested a place to camp and live in the city. Affordable housing was not available for them; therefore the city offered a location near the Portland airport (next to the prison) by the Columbia River. While this was a safe place to live, it is five miles from downtown Portland. Over the years the village, along with the help of many community volunteers, has formed a democracy, built small tent homes, and developed a system to pay the city for insurance and waste disposal. The village has provided a transitional-living community for the homeless who are trying to leave the streets and get into affordable housing or receive aid. We who are Agape Church of Christ were able to mobilize over one hundred thirty volunteers to help turn forty of their tents into walled structures. The city fire marshal worked with us to keep the villagers safe in their community. The city leadership continues to struggle to work with this village. However, many faith based and local organizations know that these are God's children in need of hope, support, and encouragement.

The first three years that Agape existed, we cultivated a strong relationship with Dignity Village. Many of the village members came to Agape and later moved into permanent housing. They worked with us in our recovery and homeless ministries and have been a valuable resource in helping people heal. Over the years, I have spent time in the village meeting, working, and eating with the members of the community. We have had Bible studies in this community as well as long conversations with the villagers. I have learned a lot about what dignity really means. It is more than a title of a community; it is something all people deserve in life.

The village people (as we call them) suffer from displacement experienced through homelessness, shame, powerlessness, and fear. Imagine what it is like to lose your job, then your home, then your family, and finally your sense of dignity. Women who live below the poverty level suddenly lose their husbands, face an illness, incur enormous hospital bills, and end up on the streets. While they are on the streets, alcohol, narcotics, and/or prostitution may briefly seem to take away the pain, shame, and emptiness. Selling sex for money pays the bills or feeds one's addiction. Women and children typically receive government aid and housing quicker than males or single females. Men who lose their jobs, families, and homes feel like they have no place in the male world. It's a form of emasculation. Everyone suffers.

Many who find their way to Dignity Village have no community, resources, or help to overcome addictions. They represent a people living in exile in one of the most beautiful cities in the United States. They are on the fringes of society geographically and socially. However, the village provides a sense of hope and community for people on the margins of my society. For those of us at Agape and other churches, it provides a window into a world of exile, displacement, and captivity.

In the beginning I had helped some of the college students deliver Taco Bell food to the community on Wednesday nights. The village people nicknamed me Pastor Taco. I prayed with many of them and became friends with some of the people. I was once asked to do a funeral for one of the women leaders who had died. She had been one of the original founders of the community and was Jewish. At the funeral I shared with mourners the statements of community members about displacement and feeling in exile. I read some of the Scriptures from the prophets and how they had an opportunity to cultivate a vision of hope and of what could be. One of the men afterward stood up and said, "One of the best things I appreciated about Sue was that she was generous with her whiskey and her pot. Like the good pastor said, we all need to stick together and help each other have something good to look forward to." I just smiled and winked at some of the Agape folks who were at the funeral. We all laughed. We understand that in exile and displacement, people struggle to find a way and use what they have at their disposal to create a vision of hope, no matter if it's a hallucination or a dream.

In the United States the American Dream includes owning a home. Those who do not own a home rent, live with their families, or live on the streets. To be homeless in a country where a common dream is to own a home is to become marginalized. Laura Stivers has suggested that the American Dream not only includes owning property but insinuates that those who own property are viewed as stable, affluent, and ethical. Conversely, those who choose not to embrace the American Dream are considered to have moral failings. Not owning a home is assumed to be a choice rather than the result of living in a society that does not "count the cost of living the American Dream." Stivers goes on,

> Clearly, the economic crisis that began in 2008 has increased the number of people who are homeless.
>
> Multiple economic and social factors have precipitated a steady decline over the last thirty years in the standard of living of poor and working-class people (and even a substantial number of middle-class people). The proverbial American Dream is out of reach for increasing numbers of Americans as job security has become more tenuous, pay and benefits have decreased, and costs of basic goods like housing and healthcare have risen exponentially.[1]

To be homeless entails more than not owning property. Being homeless carries stigma, a label, and is considered a sickness within our culture. The sickness is not the homeless people. The sickness is the existence of homelessness in our country.

Homelessness exists because affordable housing does not. "There is one starkly devastating fact that cannot be denied. If there are more people who are homeless or at risk of being homeless than there are houses, apartments, and rooms to provide them shelter, there is a crisis. And if the discrepancy between available affordable housing and the number of

1. Stivers, *Disrupting Homelessness*, 2.

people in need continues to grow, then the crisis only deepens. This is the North American situation: as the number of needy people increases, the stock of affordable housing decreases."[2]

To this looming crisis the response from many Americans, and unfortunately from many Christians, is to provide shelter for those on the streets. However, shelters are overcrowded and substandard to even the United Nations' requirements for refugee camps.[3] Homelessness strips individuals of boundaries. To be homeless in a country where the American Dream is to own a home is a form of exile. Those in poverty are many times considered to lack morals or a work ethic, and are thought to be irresponsible, struggle with personal identity and safety, and unwilling to embrace "normal standards of living." Poverty (and those who live in poverty) has been feminized, dehumanized, and demonized.

When the Occupy Wall Street movement began in Portland, many of our Agape people visited the Portland camp while some lived there. Doing ministry in this camp was a time to listen and act nonjudgmentally. People, including city officials, were in transition. It was a time when groups claimed the right to the city and the right to challenge the American Dream with its promises of security, affluence, and protection. Those on the margins challenged those with power over rights to public space, public voice, and public opinions.[4] Don Mitchell suggests that while the city is controlled by financially elite individuals, the threat of chaos is an ever-present fear for most citizens. The city as a public space for all, if it loses control to the masses, becomes a location for dialogue, conflict resolution, and questioning of the status quo.

Living in exile is a common experience for many in America who do not bow down to modern Babylon. However, exile can be a time of despair. Steven Bouma-Prediger and Brian Walsh write, "If home is a resting place, a place of security and comfort, exile is the deepest and most devastating experience of homelessness."[5] However, memory, self-dignity, and community become powerful methods to cope with the pain of exile, displacement, and marginalization. Shared pot and whiskey do

---

2. Bouma-Prediger and Walsh, *Beyond Homelessness*, 97.

3. Ibid., 46. The UN requires refugee camps to have 4-1/2 to 5 meters squared of space per person. Compare this to shelters, which provide much smaller and many times no private space.

4. Mitchell, *The Right to the City*, 7, 13.

5. Bouma-Prediger and Walsh, *Beyond Homelessness*, 20.

PART ONE Introduction: The God of Hope

not provide a house but do provide temporary relief from the shame and sadness of exile. In a sense they provide home for some.

God's People Taken Captive

In the early days of biblical Israel, there were no kings. God ruled the tribes and used prophets or seers and priests to lead and guide the people. Samuel was a prophet who called people to trust and obey Yahweh. However, God's children were rebellious and stubborn. The people of Israel asked for a king, like the surrounding peoples had, especially the Philistines. In 1 Sam 8:1–22 both Samuel and God were grieved that the people requested a human representation of a king rather than being content with God as their ruler. Yet God granted them a king named Saul, a tall man who proved to be a great warrior. As king, he struggled with pride, arrogance, and a violent temper. God later rejected Saul and chose David, the shepherd who killed the Philistine giant, Goliath, in battle. David was a man after Yahweh's heart and was both a great warrior and effective king. He united the tribes of Israel into one kingdom. In spite of his sins, the kingdom prospered under his leadership.

After David died, his son Solomon followed as ruler and was labeled "the wisest king the land had ever had." However, Solomon had seven hundred wives and concubines, who turned his heart to other gods. He was also arrogant and greedy, and he heavily taxed his people. Yahweh sent a prophet to tell Solomon that his kingdom would be divided because his heart was not devoted to God. His son Rehoboam later became king and threatened to increase the heavy taxes and abused his people (1 Kgs 12:8–11). This opened the door for further exploitation of God's people, which had begun under his father, Solomon.[6] The people rebelled and followed Solomon's commander Jeroboam, who won over ten of the tribes to the north to create the northern kingdom, called Israel.

Jeroboam likely demotivated the people of Israel from returning to Jerusalem, in Judah, by placing golden calves, idols worshiped by the Egyptians, in the cities of Dan and Bethel. These calves were similar to the one worshiped early during the Israelites' wilderness period, at Sinai (Exodus 32). The spiritual decay of the northern kingdom of Israel began, and contributed to the animosity between north and south in the biblical

---

6. Howard-Brook, *"Come Out, My People!"* 103.

history. Throughout time the Israelite kings continued to rebel against God, worship idols, and practice the "sins of Jeroboam."

Rehoboam retained the remaining two tribes (Benjamin and Judah) as well as the priestly tribe of Levi at Jerusalem. Some of the Judean kings followed Yahweh, while others, like those of the northern kingdom, rebelled against Yahweh. Those kings that turned to God focused on teaching the law (Torah), restoring the Passover feast, removing false gods, helping the oppressed, or promoting economic reform. The greatest king of this period, Josiah, removed all idols, restored the Passover, reestablished the temple, and turned his heart to the law of God (2 Kgs 23:25). Josiah was the last good king, and after his death God allowed Jerusalem to slowly deteriorate.

The kingdoms of Israel and Judah were located in a very convenient area of the ancient Near East. The coastal highway to the west of Israel, called the Via Maris, was an important roadway connecting Egypt and the Northern Fertile Crescent.[7] To the south was the mighty Egyptian empire that ruled much of the Near East for centuries. Even though the Israelites had been led out of Egypt by Yahweh, they tended to turn to Egypt for guidance, help, and military support. Solomon developed strong ties with the Egyptians through marriage and by hiring Egyptian scribes and officials to serve in his court. He also developed relationships with other kingdoms as he built Yahweh's temple. While we typically believe that the Bible writers were bragging about Solomon's glory, it is possible that Solomon was critically being compared to other Egyptian kings (including the pharaoh in Exodus).[8] This comparison narrative would suggest that Solomon's greed and power further oppressed the Israelites and fulfilled Samuel's warnings (1 Sam 8:10–18). Samuel warned the Israelites that appointing a king would turn their kingdom into a community where they would be taxed, oppressed, and exploited for his glory, rather than Yahweh's. Egypt maintained strong relational ties with Israel in order to strengthen their influence in Western Asia. Kings from both the northern and southern kingdoms relied on Egyptian power in their political relationships.

The kingdoms to the north of Israel fought over these regions and at times tried to oppose Egypt for control of the Middle East. Israel was composed mainly of small farming communities of one hundred to two hundred fifty people, but the natural barriers (hills) of Palestine allowed

---

7. Matthews, *Social World of the Hebrew Prophets*, 4.
8. Howard-Brook, *Come Out, My People*, 111–13.

PART ONE   Introduction: The God of Hope

small groups to vie for power.⁹ While the Philistines dominated the coastal region and proved to be a thorn in Saul's and David's flesh, the Syrians began a reign of terror in the north.¹⁰ Through time, the Assyrians overthrew Syria and expanded their empire. Having a one-thousand-mile territory to patrol, the Assyrians used fear to maintain their borders.¹¹ Conquest texts have been written by these kings, which describe graphic battle stories, torture, and disposal of dead bodies.¹² These texts were designed to instill fear in the inhabitants and enforce compliance. They also were a form of propaganda that targeted newer countries and used fear to coerce them into submission.

The Assyrians eventually attacked both Samaria and Jerusalem. The Jerusalem king, Hezekiah, turned to Yahweh, who intervened and protected the city. However, Samaria received the reward for their stubbornness toward God and was sacked in 721 BCE. The Assyrian king, Shalmaneser, crushed the city and took the inhabitants captive to Nineveh. The common practice of the Assyrians, and later the Babylonians, was to enact mass deportations of supplies, topsoil, and people to fund and support their ever-growing empires.¹³ They attempted to destroy the city, memory, and culture of a people that rebelled. The city of Samaria was repopulated with outsiders and later became a place with many temples and shrines to gods other than Yahweh. The city ceased to be purely Israelite and at the beginning of the first century CE, Samaria was known as a mixed breed of people who had lost their Israelite heritage. Samaria was also known as a community that lost its identity with God and its inheritance in the kingdom. Israel was punished because they had rejected Yahweh.

> All this happened because the Israelites had sinned against Yahweh their God, who had brought them up out from Egypt and the power of Pharaoh king of Egypt. They worshiped other gods and followed the practices of the nations Yahweh had driven out before them, as well as the practices that the kings of Israel had introduced. The Israelites secretly did things against Yahweh their God that were not right . . . They worshiped idols,

---

9. Matthews, *Social World of the Hebrew Prophets*, 1, 6.

10. Nemet-Nejat, *Daily Life in Ancient Mesopotamia*, 38–39.

11. Matthews, *Social World of the Hebrew Prophets*, 6.

12. Irvine, *Isaiah, Ahaz, and the Syro-Ephraimitic Crisis*, 32–39; Bleibtreu "Grisly Assyrian Record," 52–61, 75.

13. Smith-Christopher, *Biblical Theology of Exile*, 50.

though Yahweh had said, "You shall not do this" . . . But they would not listen . . . They rejected God's decrees and the covenant their fathers had made and the warnings given them . . . Yahweh rejected all the people of Israel; by afflicting them and giving them into the hands of plunderers, to send them away. (2 Kgs 17:7–23)

After taking Samaria, Shalmaneser decided to attack Jerusalem. This city was an important bridge between the Assyrian north and the Egyptian south. Jerusalem also provided resources that were necessary for Assyria to successfully defeat Egypt. King Hezekiah sought God during this time and found deliverance because of his faith. The Assyrian empire threatened Jerusalem occasionally but found their hands full with other kingdoms. Through time the fast rising power, Babylon, joined forces with the Medians to attack Nineveh.[14] Nabopolasar, king of Babylon, and his warrior son Nebuchadnezzar, followed the Median forces, who destroyed Nineveh in 614 BCE.[15] As Nineveh fell, a tremendous vacuum was created in the Fertile Crescent. All eyes were on Babylon and Egypt. While other countries chose sides or scrambled for power, the city of Jerusalem lay out of the spotlight for a short time.

The remaining kings (sons of Josiah) were puppets of either Egypt or Babylon until Nebuchadnezzar broke through the city walls at Jerusalem in 598 BCE. Josiah's son Jehoahaz was placed on the throne and ruled for three months until Pharaoh Neco removed him, carried him to Egypt, and put his brother Eliakim in charge. Eliakim later changed his name to Jehoiakim. After eleven years Nebuchadnezzar captured the city, removed Jehoiakim, and took a large portion of the Jewish population to Babylon. Jehoiakim's son Jehoiachin was placed on the throne by the people of Judah. Three months later Nebuchadnezzar removed him and took a second group to Babylon. He placed Josiah's third son, Zedekiah, in charge. Eleven years later Zedekiah rebelled against Nebuchadnezzar, and Jerusalem was destroyed. The temple was also destroyed along with the walls of the city (587/6). Jerusalem had experienced three captivities and was finally left in ruins. The final captivity came after the remaining residents of Jerusalem assassinated the political representative, Gedaliah, left by Nebuchadnezzar as a leader and community advocate over what remained of the territory.

---

14. Arnold, "What Has Nebuchadnezzar to do with David?" 349.
15. Nemet-Nejat, *Daily Life in Ancient Mesopotamia*, 43.

PART ONE   Introduction: The God of Hope

Jerusalem was the victim of a brutal rape, beating, and destruction. Those who survived barely lived as squatters. Those who were exiled, carried the pain and shame as aliens.

God's People in Exile

The biblical texts give us information not only concerning why God's people went into exile, but how the experience affected them. Reflections of Israel's emotions while in captivity are expressed in various Biblical texts. The people of God experienced their displacement through trauma, confusion, grief, and a feeling of "home-sickness" while in captivity.

First, *confusion* was one emotion experienced by the people of Judah after the destruction of Jerusalem. The people claimed that "the fathers have eaten sour grapes and the children's teeth are irritated" (Ezek 18:2; Jer 31:30). Jeremiah suggested that the people wondered why God had stopped blessing them. The book of Isaiah indicated this as well: "Look down from heaven and see, from your throne, holy and glorious. Where are your zeal and strength? Your tenderness and compassion are withheld from us. But you are our Father . . . you, Yahweh, are our Father; our ancient Redeemer is your name. Why, Yahweh, do you make us wander from your ways and harden our hearts so that we do not respect you?" (Isa 63:15–17). The people, even though they knew that they had sinned against God, believed that they were being punished for their parents' sins. Other texts suggest that the people cried out to God and were distressed because God did not save them (Jer 11:11–13, 14:11–14). Where is Yahweh?, why didn't God save us?, and, why are we in this foreign land? were common questions that they asked each other (Pss 42–43; 137; Ezek 18:2; Jer 31:30; Lam 1:9). In spite of their awareness of sin and that their suffering was punishment for it, still their overwhelming sense of suffering added to their confusion about God's power, love, and justice.

Second, the Judahites were *deeply traumatized* by their experiences. Witnessing the slaughter of their families and community as well as the destruction of their temple must have been a horrible experience. Transfer to a strange city and enslavement also took their toll emotionally on the survivors. It is likely that many of the young males who had been among the elite in Judah were castrated and brainwashed to be loyal Babylonian servants and worshipers of foreign gods (2 Kgs 19:25; Dan 1:1–7).[16] The

---

16. Wiseman, *Nebuchadrezzar and Babylon*, 84.

loss of family, faith, community, city, and identity would have scarred all of them deeply. Words used in the Hebrew Bible to describe the captivity suggest that this event was deeply traumatic.[17]

Third, this trauma and loss would have brought *grief and shame* upon the survivors. For instance, the death of Ezekiel's wife symbolized the loss of the Jerusalem temple; yet God would not let Ezekiel grieve his loss (Ezek 24:15–24). This prohibition of mourning would have brought an emotional burden on the prophet as well. In the book of Lamentations the writer expressed sadness, guilt, and fear (Lam 1:16). To encounter these biblical psalms and laments is to encounter tears, sadness, depression, agony, and despair.

Fourth, the survivors *were angry* because they felt forsaken and abandoned by God. They expressed anger over the taunting of their captors and anger over the loss of loved ones. These expressions were the stages of grief that the captives experienced (Pss 42–43; 137). They were in denial about their sin until the prophets challenged them. Like any grieving client, the people of Judah transferred their rage to their loyal therapist/prophet, and to God. However, Yahweh continued to confront them through prophets: advocates who did not back down, who met grieving Judah face-to-face, who met raw emotion with faith and obedience (Ezek 2:3–8; Jer 1:17–19).

Finally the captives from Judah experienced *displacement and homesickness*. Displacement occurs when people are traumatized through the loss of their homes, identity, stability, and sense of history. Displacement creates a longing for that identity or home (commonly called homesickness). Even though their new location was to be their home and refuge (Jer 29:7–9) the people of Judah expressed despair because of their displacement: "By the rivers of Babylon we sat and wept when we remembered Zion . . . How can we sing songs of Yahweh while in a foreign land?" (Ps 137:1, 4)

The biblical texts indicate that the captivity, while a punishment from Yahweh had a deep psychological affect on the people.

Frank Ames writes

> Exile has cascading effects. Forced relocation diminishes access to resources, which decreases the security of individuals and families and increases the incidence of disease and death . . . The

---

17. Garber, "Vocabulary of Trauma," 312–18; and Balentine, "Prose and Poetry of Exile," 348–50.

deprivations of exile include change of location and loss of property, security, and people. These deprivations have an impact on the identity and ideologies of exiles and exilic communities, which experience and increase in extended families and inclusive marriages and the embrace of supporting ideologies. Ideology yields to the pragmatics of survival. The cascading effects of exile that begin with diminished resources lead to new identities.[18]

Further, Jacob Neusner asserts, "Religion responds to historical crisis because it forms a critical component in the shaping of the public order of society and culture. Forming and re-forming a religious community embodies what people do together to solve problems, and thus the political decision of the group flow from their religion."[19] God claimed responsibility for the destruction of Jerusalem, however it was an act of "giving the Judahites what they wanted," by allowing Babylon to take the city: "Who handed Jacob over to become loot and Israel to the plunderers? Was it not Yahweh, against whom we have sinned? For they would not follow God's ways; they did not obey the law. So burning anger was poured out on them, the violence of war. It enveloped them in flames, yet they did not understand; it consumed them, but they did not take it to heart" (Isa 42:24–25). As Carleen Mandolfo has suggested, Yahweh was responding out of anger due to the deep hurt Judah had caused to this God of love and passion. "Thus, YHWH's tirades seem more the consequence of hurt than anger. He has been passed over for 'lovers' that appear to the woman, at least, to be better providers."[20]

While the prophets guided the people to reflect on their sin and repent, the community was traumatized and suffered displacement, despair, grief, and anger. They were vulnerable to disease and mental illness. The prophet was also called to confront the people and help the community heal, develop a new identity, and revive their hope. The captivity was more than a punishment; it was a time to re-orient the people to a life in God's kingdom. As the Exodus and forty-year wandering in the wilderness were a time to meet Yahweh, the seventy-year captivity was a time to reflect on their relationship with God and seek reconciliation. Their repentance demanded more than saying, "I'm sorry," or confessing guilt. Their repentance involved an emotional and spiritual transformation. The oppressors became the victims, the powerful became vulnerable, the

---

18. Ames, "The Cascading Effects of Exile," 185.
19. Neusner, *Transformations in Ancient Judaism*, 1.
20. Mandolfo, *Daughter Zion Talks Back*, 35.

wise became ignorant, the proud experienced shame, those with a history and genealogy became aliens and strangers, and those with a home embraced homelessness. In a word, they experienced the pain of Yahweh and became victims.

They also experienced the oppression that they had used to oppress others (Isa 1:21–23; 58:3–10). As they had alienated their Lord, so they became aliens. Not only had they oppressed their fellow Jews, they oppressed their God. They, like Yahweh before the destruction of the holy city, now knew what it was like to be vulnerable, hope for change, long for relationship, and feel rejection, regret, confusion, and anger.

While the people blamed Yahweh for this disaster, the prophets reminded them that they had chosen the ways of Egypt, Assyria, Babylon, and other rebellious Judeans. Their confidence was to develop from their relationship with God, not their wisdom and political values. "This is what Yahweh says: 'Let not the wise boast of their wisdom or the strong boast of their strength or the rich boast of their riches, but let the one who boasts boast about this: that they have the understanding to know me, that I am Yahweh, who exercises kindness, justice, and righteousness on earth, for in these I delight,' declares Yahweh" (Jer 9:23–24). Their punishment was actually permission to "indulge in their sins"; however their foreign relationships were painful and abusive. Yahweh allowed them to develop relationships with those who would violate them, and the price was slavery, shame, and abuse. As a victim sets the spouse free to pursue affairs and dysfunction, or as a father lets his children stay in jail for an offence, so God set Judah free to chase its lovers. What usually happens occurred also in this case: when the affair ended, the abuser was left alone, empty, and full of regret. The abuser remembered how good it was and begins to seek reconciliation with the victim. However, the abuser is responsible for this suffering, not their spouse.

The prophets were there to remind the people of the way of repentance. Like intervention counselors, the prophets in the first few decades of the eighth century BCE spent time confronting Israel with its sin. The prophets, like good and patient counselors, felt the brunt of Israel's anger. By the sixth century BCE, Jerusalem's constant rebellion became a "deal breaker" for Yahweh. Given the exchange of shared emotion, the sessions between Jerusalem captives and the prophet took their toll on both, yet Yahweh called the prophets to continue the sessions by hardening Ezekiel's forehead; by delivering and resending Jeremiah; by inspiring Habakkuk, Haggai, Zephaniah, and others. In every case the prophet wept with his patients, suffered through their trauma, cried out to God for justice and mercy for the people, and occasionally reminded them that they got what they wanted. (I wonder how often the prophets wanted to cancel the sessions with their clients, but only Jeremiah had the luxury of a secretary, [Jer 36:4].) Prophets represented the Almighty God, who also suffered with the children of Israel. However, the interaction between prophet and community was Yahweh's conduit for confronting the people.

Healing progressed slowly. Intervention proved effective. Leaders such as Daniel arose, (after reading Jeremiah's notes), confessed the sins of the people, and repented before God. Daniel's friends Hananiah, Mishael, and Azariah refused to compromise their loyalty to Yahweh. Esther, Ezra, Mordecai, and Nehemiah shouldered the burden of leadership in their homes and foreign cities. The people moved forward, survived, and returned home because a remnant of faithful ones led the way to repentance.

The Babylonian captivity was more than "punishment"; it was an intervention and act of love, by a God who needed the children to feel the pain of rejection and grief. The earlier wandering in the wilderness after the exodus had been a chance to meet Yahweh and embrace this loving, passionate God. The Babylonian captivity was a similar experience to the wilderness wandering—only this time the passionate and loving God was hurt and rejected, and needed to be validated by rebellious Israel. Working with families and individuals who struggle against domestic and sexual abuse, pornography, sexual addictions, and sex trafficking/prostitution, I have found that for the oppressors, repentance requires intervention. Those who abuse and exploit do so because they lack empathy and compassion for vulnerable others. In some cases hearing victims' stories and becoming aware of the effects of their destructive behavior become a powerful tool in repentance. Victims also need validation, support, and the chance to vent their feelings. This is important in order for oppressors to reach repentance so that forgiveness can bring healing to both.

In our work with a new church, Agape Church of Christ, we have spent energy ministering to various people in Portland. In addition to college students, professors, and young singles, we have been blessed to work with the homeless, with the sexually and otherwise physically abused, with males and females in or leaving prostitution, with recovering drug addicts, and with street kids. Many of our people have experienced displacement. I find that they have helpful insights into the emotions of captivity. While many are victims, some have made choices that have put them where they are. Yet no matter how they ended up in exile, their feelings about it are similar. Guilt, shame, grief, trauma, despair, and displacement bring all these constituencies together. To be homeless, to be displaced, and to be without history is a painful and emotionally draining experience that follows one for many years.

Exiles without Homes

Exiles and those on the margins of society have found multiple ways to resist colonization. Through literature the exiles from Judah resisted their captors and those who caused exile. Laments were oral creations that sought to stir the emotions, such as nostalgia and sorrow, among the exiles because of their displacement and punishment.[21] Reflecting on Yahweh's covenant, the Torah, and Israel's history through the literary texts was also a form of resistance. The people redefined their belief system.[22] Jacob Neusner also suggests that expressing religious faith aids in defining who an exiled community is.[23] Exile not only emotionally affects communities, but it causes communities to respond as if their exile is a calling, identity, and new community.

> When a social group shares a particular collection of written works, the group memory shaped by these texts through the very act of reading and rereading them creates a sense of identity and continuity with the past; and the same holds true for the group's recollection of text-based speeches they have heard. If the material presence of such books conveys a sense of the presence of divine teaching, and even the presence of the divine itself, among the literati, then it is reasonable to assume that the public reading of portions of the text could have had comparable effects.[24]

---

21. Smith-Christopher, *A Biblical Theology of Exile*, 47.
22. Ibid., 25–26. See also Klein, *Israel in Exile*, 14.
23. Neusner, *Transformations in Ancient Judaism*, viii.
24. Ben Zvi, "Introduction," 18–19.

PART ONE   Introduction: The God of Hope

DISPLACED AMONG THE LIVING

"Hi, Megan," I said one Sunday morning. "I'm glad you are visiting with us today. It's good to see you here for our Friend's Day. I noticed on your visitor card that you wanted prayer for some things."

She smiled and seemed somewhat timid. I guess high school kids feel a little uncomfortable when the minister comes to talk with them.

"Is it OK that I wrote those things, pastor?"

"Well, let's see. I think what you wrote is real, and I am sure that it took a lot of courage to write that."

Megan had written that she was in a support group for alcohol, abuse, self-injury, and problem behavior. I noticed that her wrists were covered and that she pulled them close to her body as she stared at the floor.

"Do you cut?" I said softly.

She nodded.

"I know why. In fact have you heard the song by Three Days Grace— 'Pain without love pain I can't get enough . . . '?"

She looked up and her eyes sparkled. "You know them? Yes I know that song."

"How about Papa Roach's *Last Resort*: 'Don't care if I cut myself bleeding'?" I asked.

"Yes, yes," she smiled, "but I really identify with Broken Home . . ."

"That makes sense," I said. "I guess you have a lot of pain and it comes from your home life?"

She nodded her head and smiled, and we talked for a few more minutes about her support group, friends, and healing. She shared with me that she had never heard a minister or church talk about "cutting," let alone about rock music. I told her that sometimes musicians are more in tune with people than our churches and Christian leaders.

Most of the bands I had followed in my earlier years were steeped in drugs, alcohol, and misogyny. However, as the 1990s and twenty-first century dawned, these composers began to do something that changed their lives, music, and messages. Rehab! Rehab has a powerful effect on an addict. Rehab is driven by one of the mighty steps of "making amends." Papa Roach proclaims the pain of broken homes, addiction, father wounds, and self-injury. Three Days Grace describes self-inflicted pain, fear, and the confusion of pain and love. System of a Down laments the suffering of a generation ruled by anger, violence, and fear. Creed, Alter Bridge, and other bands share messages of hope for those in darkness, despair, shame, and addictions. While not the most popular bands, they do form a connection with many youth living at the margins of life. Rehab has a powerful affect on the individual. Some rock musicians have begun to describe spiritual and faith experiences; they are prophets to a generation suffering from the excesses of the 1980s and 1990s (or from the excesses of their parents).

Unfortunately many of our churches cannot be prophetic because they, unlike our media and musicians, have little understanding of what marginalized people truly experience. Many people today understand exile, displacement, captivity, and spiritual or emotional homelessness. Many popular bands describe a life damaged by an abusive, absent, and uncaring parent. For many people today home is not home. In our work in Portland we not only see lives damaged by addiction, trauma, wounds, and poverty, but we see others who work to make others believe that their lives are worth saving. Contemporary prophets provide messages of hope to a nation struggling to reach stability in spite of mobility, broken relationships, abuse, addiction, and pain.

Home is a place of permanence, a place with history, a safe space, a place of love and belonging. Many people in our world lack a place to call home by this definition. For instance, immigrants leave their homes with a hope of returning one day. Refugees are driven from their homes, not knowing if they can return. Whether homeless due to their own choices or those of others, these suffer displacement. Those labeled homeless often are not only houseless; they have lost their sense of belonging. Putting these folks in a dwelling doesn't change who they feel they are. They live on the margins of society. They have been displaced.

Today's homeless, like many of us, are spiritual exiles. Like the ancient Judeans, the homeless among us in live exile (Jer 29:7–10). Exiles are captured, taken from their homes, and spend their days lamenting the shame and loneliness of separation. "If home is a resting place, a place of security and comfort, exile is the deepest and most devastating experience of homelessness."[25] Even worse, as Smith-Christopher wrote, "before any theological statement is made about exile, one must acknowledge that exile is the daily reality for millions of human beings at the opening of the twenty-first century."[26]

---

25. Bouma-Prediger and Walsh, *Beyond Homelessness*, 20.
26. Smith-Christopher, *A Theology of Exile*, 28.

PART ONE   Introduction: The God of Hope

Meanwhile, messages of false security abound in our media: Buy more stuff to be happy. Satisfy your urges and desires at any cost. Upgrade. Feel the best you can feel about yourself. However, the carriers of these messages are the false prophets of our time. They are the false witnesses of reality. Today's false prophets resemble the Jerusalem priests who, when Babylonian forces surrounded the city to destroy it, told King Zedekiah, "Have faith, God will prevail . . ." (Jer 21:1–2). Jeremiah knew it was a lie, and so did everyone else. Staring a hungry lion in the face and saying, nice kitty, has always been the role of the naïve.

Amid the false prophecies, other voices cry out for true healing. They cry out that everything is not okay. Excess is not good. Our kids need us, need love, and need a safe home. Life is worth living, and second chances exist.

- Three Days Grace cries out, "It's not too late, it's never too late . . ." Their song was accompanied by a video of a teen single mom trying to regain custody of her baby, which had been taken from her.

- Joan Osborne asked, "What if God was one of us . . . trying to make his way home?"

- Creed shared that one's own prison can be created by anger, hatred, and pain.

- Green Day suggested that the Jesus of Suburbia reflects religion's preoccupation with self rather than others.

Modern-day prophets tell us that repentance is painful but hope is real. They are preparing a generation for the future. They are calling for personal and social change. They tell us that global issues are our issues. In the end, a younger generation has risen up who care about the things I took for granted as a youth. They care about poverty, injustice, and social reform. They care about second chances. They, like the voices from rehab, believe that the world my generation is destroying is worth rebuilding.

God continues to send a message to this generation in exile. The prophets preached this message of hope, forgiveness, and empowerment. While Christianity is declining in North America and Europe, it is exploding on the continents of Africa, South America, and Asia. Even in China, where Christians can face political persecution, the underground church is multiplying. God's message to the exiles has always been the same.

First, *God seeks relationship.* Throughout the era of the prophets God wanted intimacy with Israel. Over forty-seven times God stated that the end-result of Yahweh's work would be that Israel and the kingdoms would know Yahweh as God. God has always expressed a desire to be known by people.

Second, *God offers a vision of hope.* God wanted Israel to change behavior, to come home, and to reconcile their relationship with their Lord. This vision was an alternative to what was, because God offered people what could be. The vision depended upon acceptance and obedience to God and to the vision. Sometimes the vision came true. Other times it never happened. However, the prophets continually painted a picture of an alternate ending in the midst of war, pain, and suffering. M. Jan Holton notes, "The ability to imagine a future is a lifeline for a refugee . . . Imagination is a requirement for hope. If we cannot imagine a future that opens to possibility, we fall into despair and hopelessness."[27] God always offers hope of what can be for those who are willing to believe.

The future is not always set in stone. God can change the future. God also leaves the future open based on human choices. God works with humans to accomplish the divine will. Sometimes what Yahweh wills does not happen. People make choices and can either override God's will or support it. In the time of the Hebrew prophets, God's desire was that Israel be faithful to their Lord and receive God's blessing. However, humans made bad choices and turned from their God. Therefore Yahweh allowed other kingdoms to punish Israel. This was God's will, but Yahweh's ultimate plan was not for Israel to experience exile. Exile was a consequence of their sins. God typically holds out hope of change but expects humans to partner with their Lord to fulfill these divine plans. This was displayed in Exodus when God came to rescue the people of Israel from Egypt but sent Moses to lead them out. God and Moses worked together to fulfill this plan: "I have indeed seen the misery of my people in Egypt. I have heard them crying out because of their slave drivers, and I am concerned about their suffering. So I have come down to rescue them from the hand of the Egyptians and to bring them up out of that land into a good and spacious land, a land flowing with milk and honey . . . Now the cry of the Israelites has reached me, and I have seen the way the Egyptians are oppressing them. Go. *I am sending you* to Pharaoh to bring my people the Israelites out of Egypt" (Exod 3:7–10).

27. Holton, "Imagining Hope and Redemption," 231.

PART ONE   Introduction: The God of Hope

Finally, *God initiated the conversation.* Like a father wanting to sit down with his children, so Yahweh sought opportunities to communicate with the people: "'Come now, let us settle the matter,' says Yahweh. 'Though your sins are like scarlet, they shall be as white as snow; though they are red as crimson, they shall be like wool. If you are willing and obedient, you will eat the good things of the land'" (Isa 1:18–19). Imagine God at the coffee shop sitting around a table with a group of people who are broken, suffering, and ashamed of their lives. God invites them to the table, pours them a cup of coffee or tea, and listens to them, talks with them, reasons with them, and encourages them to face their demons and stay in relationship with each other. God works with them to dream, plan, and fulfill a vision for the future. Their new life would be better, a new heavens and new earth, a time of peace, and a life of joy. God holds out this vision for people by initiating the conversation and sharing love and hope with each of us.

The message to people today is similar to the message given to the Judean captives. With those in exile God initiates conversation. For those in distress and despair God offers hope and a vision of something new, better, and more beautiful. With those experiencing guilt and shame God seeks to reestablish relationship and to bless them in their continued journey.

The message of the prophets is still a message to exiles in any generation.

3

Who Were the Prophets?

I DO A LOT of my meetings and ministry at a place in downtown Portland known as Pioneer Courthouse Square. The Starbucks on the square provides a nice atmosphere to meet people or provide a hot cup of coffee for someone holding a sign seeking money (spanging). When it is not raining in Portland, I can sit outside and visit with some of the people napping on the bench or sitting on the sidewalk across the street spanging. I meet many people at this gathering place.

One day I was walking into Starbucks and an older gentleman in a beard, with a wild look in his eyes, walked toward me, pointed his finger at me, and unleashed a barrage of cuss words and unrecognizable sounds toward me. As he drew near he shook his finger at me and cursed louder and louder. No one stopped or even noticed. It's a common event in downtown Portland. I smiled at him and made eye contact. He stopped, glared at me, and walked away talking loudly. I thought, "He is either a prophet or off his meds." Probably the latter.

Or was he the former?

What Was a Prophet?

Typically, prophets are viewed as individuals who were crazy, mystical, magicians, or on the margins of their communities. The television dramas portraying Jesus of Nazareth display John the Baptist as a loud, confrontational, and erratic preacher. Others see the prophets as fortune-tellers. In the ancient world prophets were equated with mystics, spiritists, magicians, and diviners.[1] They were preachers of God's message, not reformers of their community.[2] The Israelite prophets were distinguished by their character and work for Yahweh. Their work was contemporaneous with the monarchy, speaking to the king and court and to their God.[3] Prophets held a deep conviction that they were called by Yahweh and brought a message directly from the Lord. Many of their prophecies began with the sentence, "This is what Yahweh says," and at other times ended with, "declares Yahweh." Their courage and conviction were based not in themselves but in their calling from God.

The prophets were ordinary people. Amos and Elijah were shepherds or farmers (1 Kgs 19:19; Amos 7:14); Ezekiel, Jeremiah, and Zephaniah were priests or men associated with the court; Hosea was a scorned husband (Hos 1:2); and Samuel and Jeremiah young men apprenticed for ministry (1 Sam 3:1; Jer 1:7). Prophets were those in touch with common people. Whether they came from small towns (Jer 1:1; Amos 1:1; Mic 1:1; Nah 1:1), hailed from the larger cities (Isa 1:1; Hab 1:1; Zeph 1:1), made their homes in ruined cities (Jer 40:1; Hag 1:1; Zech 1:1), or went to foreign kingdoms (Isaiah 14–28; Jeremiah 46–51; Ezek 1:1; Jonah 1:2), these prophets knew the events of everyday life as well as the people in their neighborhoods. When Amos and Micah prophesied against the abuse of the poor and those on the margins of society, it was something they saw daily. When Jeremiah challenged the people to help the children and women of his day, he was speaking about what he saw in the streets. Judgment from Yahweh was the revelation, but the prophet described events seen firsthand. Ezekiel was the only prophet who was transported out of his community and shown the sins that occurred behind closed doors (Ezek 8:5–8).

Were the experiences of the prophets divine? Yes and no. While their call and authority came from God, the prophets described current and personal events. While the rest of the religious leaders of the day had become hardened to the daily corruption, greed, and oppression

---

1. Grabbe, "Ancient Near Eastern Prophecy," 13–32; and Matthews, *The Social World of the Hebrew Prophets*, 19–21. Matthews also writes that the equivalent for prophet (in the Mari language) was an epileptic. Egyptian hieroglyphics also describe the prophet as one having convulsions.

2. Gowan, *Theology of the Prophetic Books*, 10.

3. Petersen, *Late Israelite Prophecy*, 3.

that they saw, the prophet was *compelled by God* to speak out. Most of the experiences the prophet faced were not new, but the authority and responsibility to preach were. This is expressed in Jeremiah's complaint to Yahweh: "Whenever I speak, I cry out saying violence and destruction. The word of Yahweh has brought me insult and criticism all day long, but if I say, 'I will not speak of God or in God's name,' the word is in my heart like a fire, a fire closed in my bones. I am tired of holding it in; I cannot" (Jer 20:8–9).

The burden that Jeremiah faced was one people face when they realize that they cannot turn their heads away from injustice and oppression. It is the burden that has caused so many of us to bite our tongues and then speak out while it is swollen. No matter how hard we bite, our tongue prevails. Musicians like Bono of U2 and other social critics reveal what they see and speak out for those whom they feel are oppressed. They, like the prophets of old, share what they know and believe. They also feel a calling, an authority, and permission to call us to action. The Hebrew prophets usually preached what others already knew, but they did it with the authority and conviction from their God. They preached not only what people saw, but also what Yahweh saw. They were sent to tell the leaders that God also saw what was happening and was expressing judgment or pleasure.

Being prophetic does not mean that we preach a new revelation, a futuristic view, or hold a magical spiritual power. It is a reference to authority, calling, awareness, and a representation of God's heart. The Hebrew prophets were those who felt called to say and do something about the injustice that they saw. While their community and leaders may have been corrupt, they had encountered the Holy One, who was incorruptible. They had experienced the presence and voice of God. They knew a King whose ethic was vastly different than that of their community and leaders. They were driven by the conviction that God wanted someone to respond to what was happening. They were driven by an ethical code that told them that ignoring sin was just as wrong as practicing it. They were also driven by their own human emotions concerning the issues they faced. The prophets were emotional people who cried, shouted, screamed, cheered, and stared people down.

Leonora Tubbs Tisdale suggests that true prophets criticized the old order and energized hearers with a vision of a new reign of God that was to come.[4] The prophets were emotionally invested in their

---

4. Tisdale, *Prophetic Preaching*, xii.

community because it was *their* community. They knew the heart of God because their hearts became united with Yahweh's. They spoke for God, represented God, and in turn became more like God. To see the things that God sees may be a curse to some and a blessing to others, but it is an experience that purifies and motivates an individual to act for God. The prophetic calling was a responsibility, not a right.

When examining the literature of the prophets and their character, one can find some common qualities in their message. The prophets' messages were somehow collected by their secretaries (Jer 36:4), disciples (2 Kgs 2:3), or other scribes in the government or temple. Their words, however, were supplemented with narration, editorial comments, and poetical devices to enhance the message and prophet's authority in the Scriptures.[5] The prophetic literature and nature of the prophet had six similar characteristics.[6]

- The prophet had an intense experience of the deity.
- The prophet spoke or wrote in a distinctive way (either in prose or poetry, or sometimes in both).
- The prophet acted in a particular social setting.
- The prophet possessed distinctive personal qualities, usually defined as charisma.
- The prophet was an intermediary.
- The prophet had a distinctive message.

The prophets concerned themselves with the authority, message, and context in which they spoke.[7] The messages were not complex, exclusively futuristic, or far removed from the daily lives of their audiences. The messages were directed toward those in power, who were usually the cause of problems for the people of God and for their covenant with Yahweh. "The books of Amos, Micah, Jeremiah, Lamentations, Baruch, Habakkuk, Zephaniah, and Ezekiel have as one of their central concerns justice for those who suffer profound injustice at the hands of others whose inordinate need for power and control has caused unnecessary oppression—when Torah is disregarded, covenant is broken, God is forgotten,

---

5. Childs, *Old Testament Theology in a Canonical Context*, 122–23.
6. Peterson, "Defining Prophecy and Prophetic Literature," 33–44.
7. Matthews, *The Social World of the Hebrew Prophets*, 22–37. The prophets in the ancient city of Mari also focused on their calling rather than the character of the prophet. See Grabbe, "Ancient Near Eastern Prophecy," 29.

and the ways of justice and righteousness are abandoned."[8] The prophets were men and women called by Yahweh to act against the injustices that they had seen. They were not given a new vision but a new responsibility. They heard the judgment from Yahweh and were called to speak for God and open the eyes of others.

The prophets were part of God's divine council and dialogued with Yahweh in important decisions and actions. Messages came from the prophet and were viewed as direct commands from Yahweh (Isa 6; Amos 7:15–16). Prophets bargained with Yahweh and took part in God's decision to curse or save a community. The preexilic prophets held an important place of honor in the divine boardroom, as God sought counsel from them in helping Israel.

However, in exile things changed. First, *the prophets were removed from God's council or group of advisors.* They didn't give advice or engage in dialogue with God. They, like the people of Judah, were exiled out of Yahweh's presence. Prophecy was written down, less poetic or musical, and was mediated by angels. The prophet fully represented the people and paid the price by not being allowed into the council of God. As Meier puts it, "The fright that characteristically begins to accompany angelic revelation corresponds to the distancing of the prophets from the divine council where prophets once regularly rubbed shoulders with all varieties of supernatural creatures without any recorded discomfort. Now the appearance of a solitary figure, even in human form, is disconcerting, for prophets without access to the divine council are no longer acclimated to the rarified air of the divine realm."[9]

The prophets struggled during the exile more than before to understand God's motives as well. However, their calling was to preach to God's people and inspire new vision and hope. They were not able to see the new reality but were called to help people to envision this hope through their words and images. The exilic prophet was truly given the difficult task of inspiring helpless people to have hope in something that no one could see. The prophet was one of faith, inspiring people without vision to believe that Yahweh was a God of love and compassion.[10]

Second, *the prophets suffered with their people while in exile.* Ezekiel was a captive in Babylon. Jeremiah lived in the ruins of Jerusalem and

---

8. Dempsey, *The Prophets*, 5.
9. Meier, *Themes and Transformations in Old Testament Prophecy*, 61.
10. Tisdale, *Prophetic Preaching*, 10.

was later kidnapped (by his own people) and taken to Egypt along with his scribe, Baruch. Zephaniah describes the streets of Jerusalem as if he were running from the destruction of the Babylonian army (Zeph 1:11). Habakkuk observed the ruin of Jerusalem firsthand and cried out for mercy toward his people (Hab 1:1–3). Haggai and Zechariah returned to Jerusalem with the former exiles and helped to rebuild from the rubble of the city. The prophets were not men in ivory towers who appeared on the scene to give words of wisdom before returning to their safe gated communities. These prophets smelled the death, despair, and anger of their people. The prophets worked beside the people and saw their helplessness, fear, and discouragement in exile. The prophets also felt the brunt of people's anger for what God had them say. They also would have experienced the joy of a people hearing a message of hope and love.

Finally, the prophets of the exile, as did the prophets before them, *confronted those who abused their power*. Prophets were God's servants to balance the power of the monarchy. Theirs were the voices of justice that kept the king following God's justice. Prophets also confronted the religious leaders of the day and called them to be devoted to Yahweh. Prophets also addressed injustice in other communities outside Israel. It was extremely rare for the prophet to confront or indict the poor, oppressed, and humble of their community. Their message to these people involved hope, support, vindication, and justice. However, those who abused power were personally called to account by God's prophets. A prophet's message could be either critical or supportive, judging or inspiring, and loving or angry.

God chose prophets to represent both their Lord and community. They suffered with their community and Lord. They also bothered their people and Yahweh. The prophets were those who were true intermediaries between God and their people. They would have expressed the passion of their God and the suffering of humans.[11] One can envision the prophets preaching with pointed eyebrows, and other times standing on their toes with excitement at what God had planned for the people.

As we read the prophets, we should understand that they were human messengers. The vocabulary would at times be graphic in order to capture attention. With startling metaphors, prophets compared Israel to a prostitute, an adulteress, a pimp, a John, a violent man, a donkey, a heifer, a child, and a tree—to name a few images. "To modern audiences

---

11. Petersen, *Defining Prophecy*, 33–39.

Who Were the Prophets?

the God of the marriage metaphor may be much too violent to endure. But to Israel it was a portrait that was too honest and consistent with reality as they knew it to deny."[12]

At other times the prophet used graphic images to suggest to the people that life could be better. In Haggai God described the rebuilt temple as greater than the previous one. Archaeology suggests that the rebuilt temple was not very impressive (even King Herod later renovated the temple to make it beautiful). However, the prophets indicated that the rebuilt temple was glorious because it represented the people's second chance. It was *their* rebuilt temple and *they* were God's renewed people.

Prophets are called to intervene in their communities. Since we have planted Agape Church of Christ in Portland, I have experienced what it means to be prophetic. This time the comments come from community leaders—many who are not involved in a faith family. Over the years I have served on councils to prevent domestic violence and sexual abuse, on government agencies, and with sex-trafficking-prevention and abuse-prevention advocates. I have spoken at abuse-prevention and social-justice trainings throughout the country and have become an advocate for homeless individuals in Portland and the Pacific Northwest. I have developed relationships with people who try to call our culture to transformation. Those who serve with me have suggested that being prophetic means "getting our hands dirty," becoming advocates for the marginalized, working with civic leaders to effect change in our culture, confronting evil and oppressive systems in our communities, painting a vision of hope for others, and calling faith communities to repent and to embrace those who are oppressed.

For those in my community, then, a prophet is an advocate, a voice, and a preacher of hope and healing for those who are suffering. It is a different definition of the word *prophet* from what I have heard in the past. One definition suggests that the prophet is a troublemaker. Our other definition suggests that the prophet is a welcome voice and advocate for justice in the community. Some faith communities see a true prophet (according to our definition) as a threat—as some did in biblical history. Yet those in the community who are suffering and seeking change welcome the voice, vision, and vitality of the prophet because the prophet proclaims what might be.

---

12. Weems, *Battered Love*, 83.

PART ONE   Introduction: The God of Hope

One of our women at Agape, Senabi, is an African immigrant to the United States. Her ex-husband has spent years in prison for domestic abuse. He also decided one day during his visitation not to return their children to Senabi, and kept them from her. The police would not intervene, the children's school would not intervene, and child services would do nothing. Senabi had a court order to see the children, but no one wanted to intervene. After a long battle in court, Senabi's attorney prevailed, and the judge awarded custody to Senabi. After six months her ex-husband again withheld the children. He persuaded the same judge to award him custody. Senabi emotionally "shut down" and did not share with us for two months what happened. We again mobilized our contacts in the community and had abuse-prevention advocates and counselors helping Senabi work through the legal process to protect the children and her rights. Even the judge, who was known by our family-violence-prevention community to be supportive in abuse cases, was now siding with the husband.

I met with Phyllis, the head of the family violence council, to discuss the issue as well as the judge who had supported the ex-husband. It was a mystery to us why this had happened, but Phyllis reminded me that this is very common in our country. I knew the research presented by my friends who work in this area, and understood that batterers, sex offenders, and wealthy males typically gain custody of their children in divorce cases when they contest the case. As advanced as we are in the United States, abusive males can get their way unless the community bands together to resist them. Senabi was one of many women suffering injustice, even in "the land of the free and home of the brave." Even though her family stated that she was receiving more justice than she would have in her home country, I was convinced that what was happening was wrong. She was our sister, and we felt compelled to fight for her.

"Phyllis," I said, "I don't know what to do about this. My instruction manual says very little about working with judges who I believe are unjust."

Phyllis smiled as I said this. "I see your point, but I think your instruction book says you are doing the right thing now; you are representing her case and standing with her. You are also giving her hope."

Phyllis was right. Justice is hard work, not only for God, but God's leaders. However, we must be active in our communities and advocate for our neighbors. This takes patience, endurance, and courage.

The message and role of the prophets carry power for people today. Those who have been through rehab and put their lives back together share with me that their lives are different from before, but good. While a new life does not change or make right the old, it can provide peace and hope for the future. For those who have experienced modern exile and displacement, the prophets hold out hope for a better life. This new life is not better than it was before, but it is better than the pain of separation, suffering, isolation, and shame. It is a chance for transformation and healing. This new life is reflected in a new covenant, in the new heavens and new earth, and in a new relationship with God. The prophets, who also experienced spiritual rehab, share with God's people in the joy and hope of the new life. They also share God's message of hope, of what might be. They stand firm with a message of hope for those on the margins of our society, and with accountability for those using power over others.

The Ugandan Anglican bishop Festo Kivengere, a prophet at work, described his experiences ministering to those suffering in his war-torn country. "In the summer of 1982, my wife and I went into a camp that was not yet a camp. The refugees were standing by the river, 8,000 of them, in the rain and without any shelter. A mother delivered a baby right there in the mud. Two people died of pneumonia as I was standing there. We had no medicine, no food. We did not even know what to expect. It was heartbreaking. You stand there and you cry like a child. And you cry because you know you can't do much about it, and yet you have to give hope."[13]

This is why our world needs prophets!

---

13. Ntamushabora, *From Trials to Triumphs*, xx.

PART TWO

Advocates for Hope

4

Jeremiah

God in Therapy, Working with Both for Reconciliation

THE PROPHET JEREMIAH BEGAN his ministry as a young man. He was from the town of Anathoth, where Solomon exiled Abiathar the priest, who was from Eli's family—the priestly line in the days of Samuel. We don't know the exact age when Jeremiah was called as a prophet for Yahweh, but the book of Jeremiah tells us that he was a "youth" (Jer 1:6): "Lord Yahweh, I do not know how to speak; I am a young man." The Hebrew word *na'ar* means "apprentice" or "young man of noble birth." Jeremiah was not a child; he was a young man being trained to serve in an official capacity.[1] When God called him to publicly preach, Jeremiah was anxious about this task, but only because he did not feel ready. As an apprentice and priest's son, he knew the day would come for him to fulfill a mission for God, but it would have been an awesome calling.

---

1. For more information on the use of this word see: Hildebrandt, "Proverbs 22:6a" 3–19; MacDonald, "The Status and Role of the *Na'ar*," 147–70. The Talmud applies *na'ar* to young people between ages sixteen and twenty-four. See Plaut, *The Jewish Commentary for Bible Readers*, 227.

PART TWO   Advocates for Hope

Jeremiah was also called during the time another youth was leading the nation of Judah.[2] Josiah began his reign of Judah at age eight. When he turned twenty-one, his officials found the book of the law (probably what is now titled Deuteronomy) and read these stories to the king. Josiah's people were steeped in idolatry, violence, and neglect of God's temple; and Deuteronomy's words brought condemnation. Josiah tore his robes and enacted kingdom-wide reforms. It was during this time that Jeremiah was called to preach. Yahweh's word came to him in Josiah's thirteenth year as king (Jer 1:1).

It is hard to know whether Jeremiah began preaching before Josiah's discovery of God's law or during Josiah's reforms. God spoke through Jeremiah to address idolatry, the neglect of Yahweh, and the social injustice of the people. Josiah destroyed every idol, idol's priests and temples, and high places in his kingdom (2 Kgs 23:8–16; 2 Chr 34:33). He also was a king who took care of the poor and oppressed. Jeremiah had told Jehoahaz, one of Josiah's sons, that his father cared about social justice. "Your father had food and drink? He did what was right and just, it was good with him. He defended the cause of the poor and needy, it was good. That is what it means to know me" (Jer 22:15–16). Josiah and Jeremiah had the same goals for their kingdom and reflected the heart and passion of God for the kingdom of Judah. Both may have worked together to enact kingdom-wide reforms. It is also clear that Josiah's aids, Shaphan and Hilkiah, continued to cultivate this heart for God as their sons Micah, Gemariah, and Elishama listened to and protected Jeremiah during his later years (Jer 36:8–18). Jeremiah even wrote a lamentation for king Josiah after he died.

Jeremiah and Josiah were both young men who provided strong leadership for their God and kingdom. While Josiah carried the political power and financial backing to finish the job, Jeremiah proclaimed God's message to leaders who would listen to his words, and later to leaders who would reject God's message. God commissioned Jeremiah, in a manner similar to Josiah, by suggesting:

- I am with you
- I will give you insight into Jerusalem's future (2 Kgs 22:18–20; 2 Chr 34:27–28)

Josiah was told that he would die in peace because he showed remorse for neglecting God's law and temple. Jeremiah, however, was involved in

2. McConville, *Judgment and Promise*, 19.

the discussion with and accusations toward Judah throughout his nation's suffering and violence. Judah was guilty, and Jeremiah was sent to tell them to repent. While Jeremiah saw the sin of his people, God revealed to Jeremiah, not only their obvious sin, but Yahweh's pain because of the sin. The kingdom would not listen to God or the prophets, was worshiping other gods/idols (Jer 5:7, 23–24; 7:9), was oppressing those who were vulnerable (Jer 5:26–28; 6:7, 13; 7:5–6, 9), and were allowing their leaders to ignore God's will in their governing the people (5:4–5; 8:8–9). Judah was like a spouse who neglects, abuses, and bullies their family members. God was angry and hurt because Judah, as God's partner, was abusive and neglectful concerning their Lord's wishes. Not only were the people of Judah hurting God, but they were hurting each other.

This pattern of neglect, however, had arisen when leaders abandoned the way of God: "I said, 'These are only the poor; they are foolish, for they do not know the way of Yahweh, the justice of their God. I will go to the leaders (great ones) and speak to them since they know the way of Yahweh, the justice of their God.' But together they had broken off the yoke and their bonds" (Jer 5:4–6).

As Jeremiah moved among the people, he proclaimed God's message to an unfaithful spouse, much as a therapist would represent a victim's thoughts to an abuser and restate them during a marriage counseling session. However Jeremiah, as Yahweh's representative, fully vented the anger of his Lord, the victim. Throughout the book that bears his name, Jeremiah permitted few words from the unfaithful spouse but allowed God to vent. Jeremiah reminded the offender that God was angry enough to turn away from the partner, hand the husband a certificate of divorce (Jer 3:1–5), pour out fire/anger upon her unfaithful husband (Jer 7:20), and completely cut off his wife. Yet after the rage was expressed in the therapist's office, so to speak, God's willingness to forgive, heal, restore, and reestablish a relationship was always a possibility. At times the session involved yelling and screaming, yet at other times there were tears, tenderness, and hope. Jeremiah was the mediator and communicated that confrontation and healing were necessary for this relationship to have any hope. As Kathleen O'Connor has observed, "In YHWH's opening expressive burst of pain, first-person verbs spiral downward in the direction of despair. His cheerfulness disappears, grief descends upon him, sickness invades the heart of God"[3]

---

3. O'Connor, "The Tears of God," 398.

PART TWO   Advocates for Hope

The Intake and Setting a Course for Marriage Sessions

In the first three chapters of Jeremiah God accuses the people of unfaithfulness. In chapter 1 Jeremiah was commissioned to a task that involved Yahweh's support and encouragement. In chapter 2, God passed judgment on the nation. The people were charged with breaking the marriage relationship with God. They had been unfaithful, had forsaken their lover, and had killed God's messengers as well as the innocent poor (2:9, 30, 34). While they were charging God with wrongdoing (typically the first statement someone makes when caught cheating on their spouse—"you drove me to this . . ."), the people themselves had wronged the one who had cared for them. Even more, Yahweh claimed that Judah had turned to other lovers who did not have their best interest in mind.

I have always said that sexual affairs, pornography, prostitution, and sexual assault are rarely concerned with good looks. The hurt spouse tries to change appearances to become more appealing, but this does not change the offender's behavior. Violators of a covenant are typically so steeped in shame and sinfulness that they choose this behavior. They allow distance to accumulate between them and their partner, and through neglect, abuse, or immaturity they seek a relationship with another person. They forget, as God's ancient people did, how to feel guilt and shame. "Are they ashamed of their detestable [abomination/abominable] actions? No, they have no shame at all; they do not even know how to blush" (6:15; 8:12). God confronted Judah because they sought help from statues and idols. They had turned from fresh water to nasty cistern water (Jer 2:13); they were like female donkeys in heat, looking to mate with anything in their path (2:23–25); and they continued to live in their guilt and shame (Jer 2:22).

God was faced with a dilemma. If God divorced Judah, they could not be taken back. The land would be defiled if Yahweh reestablished a covenant with unfaithful Judah (Deut 24:1–4; Jer 3:1–2). Yet God could not tolerate this type of relationship: Judah was acting like a prostitute or an adulterous spouse, and by staying in relationship Yahweh was manifested as a pimp who allowed "his woman" to have sex with other males. For Yahweh to continue this relationship not only shamed Judah, but it dishonored God. God was not a pimp but a faithful spouse who provided, nurtured, and cared for the other. Yet, Yahweh, as a faithful spouse, expected faithfulness as well. Something had to be done for the sake of God's honor.

In our work to understand and rehabilitate intimate-partner violence (commonly known as domestic violence) and marriages in dysfunction, it is important for the hurt spouse to identify with God in the prophets. Often the faith community communicates that "there is no divorce" (even though Jesus gives permission for divorce—Matt 5:32; 19:9; Mark 10:10– 12), or that "every marriage problem can be worked out . . ." Yet few understand what a covenant relationship is designed to be. Covenant involves two faithful parties. If one party is unfaithful, then they *break the covenant* (Hebrew: *bgd*, which also means to "break faith"). So Yahweh reminds Judah that they had "broken faith" in their covenant with God (Exod 21:8; Jer 3:8; Mal 2:11). God had the option to divorce Judah or to send the people away.

When one person introduces violence, addiction, sexual unfaithfulness, or neglect into a marriage, the person "breaks faith" with the partner. Divorce happens when someone has violated their covenant. Therefore, divorce is not the problem in our society. Rather, broken faith by one of the spouses is the problem. The offended spouse always has the option to send away or reconcile, depending upon the offender's willingness to repent and make amends. The offender does not call the shots, have control, or decide the future of the relationship—the victim has the right to be honored and to decide the future of the relationship.

> You say, "I am innocent; God is not angry with me." But I will pass judgment on you because you say, "I have not sinned." (Jer 2:34–35)

> You called to me: "My Father, my companion from my youth, will you always be angry? Will your anger continue forever?" This is how you talk, but you do all the evil you can. (Jer 3:4–5)

God was going to decide the fate of Judah, not the oppressor.

God's Response

Because Judah had broken faith, God had to punish them as described in their covenant.[4] In Jer 3:8 God mentions his divorce of the kingdom

---

4. Various authors suggest that God's character is unstable, erratic, and very emotional. This is due to the treatment God received from a people loved and respected by

of Israel, who were taken captive to Assyria, and would therefore divorce Judah. God hoped that Judah would see the sin of Israel and repent, but they chose the same path. The Hebrew in Jer 3:9 reads "through the lightness of adultery," suggesting that Judah saw their unfaithfulness as insignificant.[5] However, this divorce would be a "wake-up call." God hoped that Judah would return. Yahweh would take them back, reestablish a new covenant, and bless them. God was warning them, calling them to repent, and asking for them to remember the days of their early marriage.

The next section contained prophecies, judgments, and warnings during the times of Josiah's sons (Jer 3:6—20:18). In this section Jeremiah explained why Yahweh had filed charges against the people of Judah and how dysfunctional their relationship had become. Judah was unfaithful (3:20), had worshiped other gods and sought salvation from them (3:24–35; 5:19; 7:1, 30; 11:12; 14:14; 16:13; 19:5), had lost their sense to act wisely (5:4–5; 8:8), had oppressed the poor and those depending on leaders for justice (5:26–28; 6:13 7:6; 9:8; 17:11), and had worked on the Sabbath rather than allowing people to rest (17:19–27). In this section God summarized a case against Judah: this spouse had not listened to the partner. God charged Judah with neglect (Jer 7:1). Jeremiah stood at the gate of the temple (where Josiah had enacted a massive restoration project) and proclaimed that God's people had ignored their Lord.

When Yahweh had led Israel out of Egypt, the people were encouraged to obey God. The Hebrew for "obey" is the same as that for "listen." God was less concerned about the sacrifices that they offered and more concerned with willingness to listen and obey.

> This is what Yahweh Almighty, the God of Israel, says: "Go up, add your burnt offerings to your other sacrifices and eat the meat yourselves. When I brought your ancestors out of Egypt and spoke to them, I did not just give them commands about burnt offerings and sacrifices, but I gave them this command: Obey [listen to] me, and I will be your God and you will be my people. Walk in all the ways I command you, that it may be good for you." But they did not listen or pay attention; instead, they walked by their own hearts. (Jer 7:21–24)

Yahweh had a simple request: to listen/obey. Jeremiah's sermon was conveniently given at the temple, the place where God was expected

---

their creator—a people who in turn rejected and mistreated their Lord. See O'Connor, "The Tears of God," 387, 390; McConville, *Judgment and Promise*, 72.

5. Thompson, *The Book of Jeremiah*, 196.

to encounter the people. Unfortunately the leaders and the people as a whole had learned to ignore their God, especially at the temple.

Throughout this section of Jeremiah, God reminded Judah that they were not listening to (11:19; 13:11), did not acknowledge (9:3, 6, 13), and had forgotten their Lord (13:25). God, therefore, refused to listen to, acknowledge, or remember the people.

> This is what Yahweh says: "Disaster will happen, which they cannot escape. Although they cry out to me, I will not listen. The towns of Judah and the people of Jerusalem will cry out to the gods to whom they burn incense, but they will not save them when disaster strikes. Judah you have as many gods as you have towns; and the altars you have set up to burn incense to that shameful god Baal are as many as the streets of Jerusalem. Do not pray for this people or offer any plea or petition for them, because I will not listen when they call to me in distress." (Jer 11:11–14)

> Then Yahweh said to me, "Do not pray, beg, or plead for these people to be well. Although they fast, I will not listen to their cry; though they offer burnt offerings and grain offerings, I will not accept them. Instead, I will destroy them with the sword, famine and plague." (Jer 14:11–12)

Since the people of Judah had rejected God, they would be ignored. The two passages above are very disturbing to me. First, *I was always taught that God would never ignore the cries of the children who call out to their Lord*. I was also taught that people on their deathbeds could possibly turn to the Lord and receive salvation before dying. According to these passages, God can choose to ignore people and allow them to face the consequences of their sins. As a Christian leader, I have had to come face-to-face with the fact that God will do what God wants. We cannot predict nor can we tell people what God will do in every incident. It is possible that God will say, "You will get everything coming your way and I will not bail you out." It is also possible that God will intervene. However, since God is a God of justice, I believe we can trust that God will be fair and just.

Second, *the above passages are disturbing because they challenge me as a leader to stop rescuing people*. Jeremiah would obviously be compelled out of compassion to pray for the deliverance of his people. The text assumes that he would try to intervene for his city. He, like a good therapist, would ask for another session with the client, one more chance, and the willingness of the victim to try again. He pled with God to not let go:

> "You are among us, Yahweh, and we carry your name; do not forsake us . . ." (Jer 14:9)

> "For the sake of your name do not despise us; do not dishonor your glorious throne." (Jer 14:21)

> "Therefore our trust is in you, for you are the one who does all this." (Jer 14:22)

Jeremiah cared about his people and would have seen the overwhelming judgment on this kingdom. God knew that the prophet would react out of compassion and try to save them from punishment. Yet God called him to preach rather than to save. Jeremiah was to warn his people to repent and deliver the divorce documents as they were.[6] Sometimes it is hard to warn others and confront them for their behavior. However, God calls us to this task, knowing we will be compelled to love them. Sometimes it is hard to be a prophet when you have the capacity to love and practice compassion for people. If we lacked the compassion, then we could not act in a prophetic mode.

This compassion also helps us to identify with God's passion, hurt, and desire for change. Throughout this section of Jeremiah God offered hope for change. God was going to punish the people by sending them to another nation, Babylon. God sent them prophets whom Judah rejected. Therefore, Yahweh would send them Babylon, whom they could not reject. Even though God poured out fire/wrath/anger in this punishment, the Spirit of hope and healing would later come to promote restoration (7:20). God will leave a remnant (5:18; 12:15) and give grace for them to grow again. If they were willing to change their behavior, God would provide for them and become the spouse that they had always wanted but had quickly neglected (15:19–21). God promised to bring them back to their home. They would remember God as the God of second chances: "'However, the days are coming,' declares Yahweh, 'when it will no longer be said, "As surely as Yahweh lives, who brought the Israelites up out of Egypt," but, "As Yahweh lives, who brought the Israelites up out of the land of the north and out of all the countries where God had banished them." For I will return them to the land I gave their ancestors'" (Jer 16:14–15).

---

6. McConville, *Judgment and Promise*, 62.

God had a dream, a vision, and a plan. Even though God's people would be punished for their unfaithfulness, Yahweh saw that they could become something more and could return to a healthy relationship with their God. Yahweh saw hope in that they would be taught to know and honor their God (16:21). It is this ability to hope, dream, and share the vision that drove Jeremiah to preach both judgment and hope. This hope revived as Jeremiah described what the lives of the Judahites could be. Clay to be molded has great potential (Jer 18:1–17). Therefore God would mold and forgive the nation if willing to change.

However, as Jeremiah 19 has it, many in the nation had become hardened like dried clay. The pot had to be broken or shattered for God to be honored. This shattering was illustrated when Jeremiah confronted Pashhur, one of the priests who assaulted and arrested him for speaking so negatively (Jer 20:2). Jeremiah was put in stocks or shackles near the temple, where he had given his condemning speech. Even though Jeremiah was quickly released, it was clear that some leaders were hardhearted and could only be shattered for the hope of Israel to repent. At the beginning of this section of Jeremiah, Judah, it seemed, could change and repent; however, as the prophet continued to warn, it became clear that Jerusalem did not desire to be married to Yahweh and could not repent.[7]

Jeremiah suffered not only the same neglect and rejection as his God, but also the stress of being traumatized. The hopelessness and despair of a people that would not repent affected him emotionally. He had heard God's pain, anger, and threats against his people and struggled between having the courage to speak for God and having the compassion for his city. Jeremiah was the marriage therapist who had heard one side of the story but who had seen the other firsthand. While he had observed the city and its evil, watched a king enact reforms, and lived among the city's residents throughout his life, he had, like so many of us, become numb to the hustle and bustle that goes with living in a large community. However, when God vented in Jeremiah's office, he heard the raw emotion from the Creator victimized by those created in God's image. The pain and suffering that came from betraying God resulted in anger, vengeance, and grief. Jeremiah was now listening to a God who had become vulnerable, humiliated. Because of honor, God had to respond and do what a Creator must do:

---

7. Ibid., 43.

PART TWO Advocates for Hope

> "Shouldn't I punish them for this? Shouldn't I judge a nation such as this?" (Jer 5:9, 29)
>
> "Shouldn't you [that is, the people] fear me? ... Shouldn't you not tremble in my presence?" (Jer 5:22)

Jeremiah was called to facilitate the intervention. On one side was the hurt spouse (God). On the other side was the offender who was in denial (Judah). Yet Jeremiah continued to convey the feelings and message of his God, the offended party. He began to realize that the nation was not only abusive; they chose to be in denial. "To whom can I speak and give warning; who will listen to me? Their ears are closed and they are not able to hear. The word of Yahweh is offensive to them; they find no pleasure in it. But I am full of the wrath of Yahweh, and I cannot hold it in. Pour it out on the children in the street and on the young men gathered together; both husband and wife will be caught in it, and the old, those full of years" (Jer 6:10–11). As God vented and proposed a future of punishment, death, and captivity, Jeremiah expressed his and God's grief at the loss of a relationship that had once brought joy to God as well as blessings to a nation: "Since my people are crushed, I am crushed; I mourn, and it holds me. There is no balm in Gilead. There is no physician there. Why then is there no healing for the wound of my people? My head is a spring of water and my eyes a fountain for tears! I would weep day and night for the slaughter of my people" (Jer 8:21—9:2).

However, Jeremiah had to confront the people over their denial. A good therapist is not only a good listener. An adept counselor can confront those in denial and call them to validate those they have hurt. Jeremiah the therapist had seen and heard enough of God's side of the story to know that injustice had happened. While Jeremiah's contemporary, King Josiah, enacted strong reforms that increased devotion to God, the people quickly returned to their old ways following Josiah's death. Jeremiah could not be silent and spoke out, even at the risk of being physically assaulted.

After Pashhur released him from his shackles, Jeremiah confronted him for this injustice and Judah's sins. He then admitted how difficult it was to be God's mediator: "Whenever I speak, I cry out preaching violence and destruction. So the word of Yahweh has brought me insult and rejection all day. But if I say, 'I do not remember, or I won't speak in God's name,' the word is in my heart like a fire; it's in my bones—I am tired of holding it in; I cannot" (Jer 20:8–9). Just as any overwhelmed marriage counselor might, so Jeremiah wished he had not taken on this case. However, God promised to care for him, and as any good counselor knows, it's not about the money but about the experience. Jeremiah needed to know that he was doing the right thing, and that making a difference had to begin with himself. There seemed to be little hope that Yahweh's partner would repent, yet Jeremiah was expected to do a job and keep asking Judah to return home.

Interacting with Political Officials

Jeremiah's discussions with the political leaders of Judah was also a disaster. God had vented feelings of neglect and laid the foundation for the future. Judah had been in denial, but things had to change. For Jeremiah the future was bleak. Could this relationship be salvaged? Would there be reconciliation? Would Judah repent so that God could forgive them? Could the years of hurt and pain be addressed by a people unwilling to admit their sin against their God? Would punishment work in turning them back to God? Who would survive God's discipline and who would never get another chance? The future looked bleak because it was based on God's people repenting. However, God believed that it could happen.

This section of Jeremiah begins as Zedekiah, the last king of Judah, bends Jeremiah's ear concerning the future. The Babylonian army had flexed their muscles and taken Judah's leadership to their country. Egypt and Babylon fought for control of Jerusalem and Babylon had become the victor. King Nebuchadnezzar was God's chosen one to ruthlessly punish the nation of Judah for abuses toward God. The offender was now willing to talk in the counseling sessions, so to speak.

"What do you want me to do? OK, you're right, I cheated. What of it? "I suppose you won't be happy until to you get the house, the car, the kids, and leave me with nothing . . ."

Zedekiah wanted to listen, if only for a brief period. He was facing jail time and knew that he needed to do something drastic to save his marriage.

"What do you want me to do? Stop seeing her/him? Come back home? Quit my job? Buy you something nicer? Should we go on a vacation together? Would that make you feel better?"

The damage had already been done. God had told Jeremiah that Babylon would serve the divorce papers and then trash the house. Judah

PART TWO   Advocates for Hope

and the leaders had not listened to God's warnings (Jer 21:4, 7, 8), and it was time to act. Still, after seventy years, God would establish a new covenant with a new generation. Jeremiah recounted his conversations with Josiah's other sons—with Jehoahaz (Jer 22:11–12) and Jehoiakim (22:18)—and with Jehoiakim's son Jehoiachin (22:24); yet all of the kings refused to listen to their God (22:21). Jeremiah even confronts other spiritual and community leaders (called shepherds) and the prophets who preached peace, corruption, and abuse in the land (Jeremiah 23).

In the future God would take care of the children by providing leaders (shepherds and prophets) who would protect and teach the people to listen to their God. Judah had become a basket of rotten figs, but the few unspoiled ones would be taken out and saved (Jeremiah 24). The army from the north (Babylon) was coming to make the people of Judah listen to their Lord. Judah's leaders had failed their people and their God, and Yahweh decided to care for the people who had been deceived by corrupt rulers.

Their punishment was an all-expense-paid trip to one of the most powerful and beautiful countries in the world: seventy years of captivity in Babylon. The Babylonians would break down Jerusalem and have their way with the residents. They would kidnap the rich and famous youths and take them to their home. Jerusalem would lose future leaders, its temple, its valuables, and any hope of having a future as the capital of a sovereign territory. In this divorce case, God hired the best attorneys and took them to the cleaners. Those lucky enough to live would have a new home in Babylon, a new language, and the idols and gods they so desperately wanted to have. They would be free to worship the gods who could not save them from themselves. After the people of Judah had their fill, those who lived through the exile would return home to rebuild their city (Jer 25:12 15). Those left in Jerusalem during the exile of the majority would mourn the loss of a kingdom. They would grieve the sins of their fathers and themselves.

In spite of this future, Jeremiah had worked hard to prove that God still held out hope of change. In one of his many temple sermons Jeremiah shared that there was still hope for change.

> "This is what Yahweh says: 'Stand in the courtyard of Yahweh's house and tell all the people of the towns of Judah who come to worship in the house of Yahweh everything I command you; tell them all my words. Maybe they will listen and each repent from their evil ways. Then I will have compassion/relent and not

bring on them the disaster I was planning because of the evil they have done.'" (Jer 26:2–3)

"Now change your ways and actions and listen to Yahweh your God, then Yahweh will have compassion/relent from the disaster spoken against you." (Jer 26:13)

Some suggest that once God determines something, it has to happen. Others suggest that God knows the future and cannot change it. Still others believe that God does not change the divine will. However, Jeremiah 26 and other passages indicate that God allows the future to change. Yahweh was willing, eager, and hopeful that the people would listen and pursue a change of behavior. God was willing to change the future, if the people were willing to repent. This God becomes vulnerable and takes great risks to connect with a people who were stiff necked, rebellious, and unwilling to listen. This God of second chances was willing to alter the divorce proceedings if the spouse would break off the relationship. This act of hope and trust required a God who was willing to be revictimized. It also required a God who believed change and love was possible. God hoped for a better future: "If you break off the relationship with him/her, we can start over . . ." It was the moment in the therapist's office when the offended spouse (God) was willing to offer a glimpse of hope, the ability to forgive and see that things can be better. It was the spouse's expression that divorce is not desired, that one is willing to commit to the long work of healing and to the rekindling the love that once existed. It was that moment when the therapist watched in awe as the victim offered to love and trust again.

However, God's willingness to negotiate continued to be met with resistance. "I don't want to break it off with him/her . . . ," was the reply of Judah's kings. Jeremiah proclaimed that Nebuchadnezzar would take Jerusalem (Jeremiah 27) and enslave the residents. This prophet wore a yoke around his neck (an implement used to tie farm animals to a plow). As an ox was bound to slave in the fields for a master, so the people of Judah were bound to be slaves in Babylon. Hananiah, another prophet, took the yoke from Jeremiah, broke it, and proclaimed freedom. Jeremiah returned the next day with an iron yoke, "Break this yoke, Hananiah," was the message God sent to the people of Judah.

PART TWO   Advocates for Hope

Offering Hope of Healing

Yet the divorce between God and the people was not a disaster for everyone. As a child of divorce, I understand that sometimes the dissolution of marriage brings a sense of peace and stability to the home. While it is difficult to leave a home in the suburbs and move to an apartment in a low-rent complex, life can still exist with hope, peace, and safety. God would be with those in captivity. Parents sit with their children and explain that there will be a divorce, but that the children will still be loved by mom and dad, and that life will be different and difficult. God had such a conversation. Jeremiah wrote a letter to the captives and sent it to Babylon (Jeremiah 29). Even though Nebuchadnezzar had attacked Jerusalem and taken the people captive, in Jeremiah's letter to the exiles, God claimed to be responsible for this event: "This is what Yahweh almighty the God of Israel says to those I carried into exile from Jerusalem to Babylon . . ." (29:4). The exiles were called to settle into their new city, to grow their families, and support their new government. Yahweh told them to seek the peace (*shalom*) of their city. Home was Jerusalem (Jeru-*shalom*). So Babylon, their new home, was to become their "new Jerusalem" (*shalom*). The captives were told to be leaders and good citizens in Babylon rather than rebels. The next generation would return home and reestablish their city and a relationship with their God. Maybe they would break the cycle of dysfunction and restore the honor Yahweh deserved.

Since over the course of the book of Jeremiah it becomes clear that Judah will not repent, and that they will have to make the best of their life in another country, God holds out hope for another plan. God had claimed to know the plans for the captives (Jer 29:11), which suggests Yahweh was making new plans even as the old ones were being rejected. God was dreaming of a new future that included the children of Israel. While the exiles could not see past their stubbornness, Yahweh saw change, hope, and a new future. This future was expressed in Jeremiah 30–33. If God's spouse would not look to the future and restore dignity to the family, then Yahweh will raise up a generation who will bless and honor their God. Yahweh's hope was described as a new covenant/relationship (31:33–34), as God becoming their God and they God's people (30:22; 31:1), as compassion (31:20), as restored blessings (32:38–40), and as an agreement not easily breakable (33:20–24).

> "The days are coming," declares Yahweh, "when I will make a new covenant [cut a new covenant] with the people of Israel

and Judah. It will not be like the covenant I made with their ancestors when I took them by the hand to lead them out of Egypt, because they broke my covenant, even though I was their husband," declares Yahweh. "This is the covenant I will make with the people of Israel after that time," declares Yahweh. "I will put my law in their minds and write it on their hearts. I will be their God, and they will be my people. They will not teach their neighbor, or say to one another, 'know/learn about Yahweh,' because they will all know me, from the least of them to the greatest," declares Yahweh. "For I will forgive their rebellion and will not remember their sins." (Jer 31:31–34)

"I will gather them from all the lands where I banish them out of anger and wrath; I will bring them back to this place and let them live in security. They will be my people, and I will be their God. I will give them one heart for their direction, so that they will respect me and it will be good for them and their children. I will make an eternal covenant with them: I will never stop doing good to them, and I will give them a heart to fear me, so that they will never turn away from me. I will delight in doing good to them and will place them in this land with my heart and soul." (Jer 32:37–41)

In reading this text it seems that Yahweh was naïve and willing to believe in a pipe dream. How can God expect stiff-necked humans to be loyal? God concluded that humans were evil from youth (Gen 8:21) and stiff-necked continually. God cannot change people, yet God offers the future generation an everlasting and unbreakable covenant/marriage (Jer 31:31–34). However, the language was not one meant to be literal. It was the language of love, hope, and passion. God was speaking to the unfaithful spouse as one trying to win a heart: "You think you are loved by him/her? I love you more, and I will fight for you. You think you have a future with them? When they leave you, where will you be? I will always be there and even now, I am willing to make it work!" This is the language of a God who is passionate for people and relationships. This God does not believe in a pipe dream, but a glimpse into what could be, what might be, what God longs to see. This vision was so beautiful that Jeremiah interjected into the vision, "At this I woke and looked around. I had a pleasant night's sleep" (Jer 31:26).

God gave this vision in spite of the corrupt leadership that tried to squelch God's passion. After the vision of a new relationship the book of Jeremiah moved into the prophet's conflict with the religious leaders.

PART TWO   Advocates for Hope

King Zedekiah continued to waver about whether to obey God or listen to his "positive thinking" priests. He cheated the slaves and debtors out of their freedom and safety (Jeremiah 35). The Recabites, a clan committed to their traditions and their faith, were powerful witnesses to a life of obedience toward God. Yet Jehoiakim would not learn from their example and continued to give God the finger (Jeremiah 35). In addition, King Jehoiakim, unlike his father, read Jeremiah's sermon (which the prophet's secretary, Baruch, had written down) and instead of tearing his robes (as his father Josiah had done) Jehoiakim tore and cut the document, throwing it in the fire (Jeremiah 36). Jeremiah was thrown into prison, beaten, and then ignored by his kings and the leaders in Jerusalem.

However, a few faithful leaders and servants protected this man of God. After Jerusalem was destroyed, the remaining Jews ignored God's pleas to repent. In light of all that had occurred they claimed that their misfortune happened because they had neglected the goddess Asherah, whom they called the Queen of Heaven (Jeremiah 44). Instead of returning to the therapist's office to work through the divorce, they complained that they had missed out, married too young, and needed a few more sexual encounters to find themselves. It was one more slap in God's face and one more reason Jeremiah struggled to advocate for the nation. Jeremiah and his secretary, Baruch, were taken hostage by the people (just in case the captors needed a counselor to work through any future issues), to Egypt where God promised to send Babylon. Jeremiah, like Moses, had preached to the people for forty years. But unlike Moses and the Israelites, who had left Egypt in the exodus, Jeremiah was exiled back to Egypt. Judah's remnant had returned to the land of slavery to escape the God who had led them from Pharaoh.

A Warning to the Neighborhood

Obviously the neighbors would ask questions. When the neighborhood heard the door slam and witnessed the man across the street picking up his clothes and belongings that had been thrown into the yard, they knew that something bad had happened. When his wife hurled the television set out the window and onto the sidewalk, they knew that he had hurt his wife. He was kicked out of the house. She would not tolerate any more bad behavior. When the neighborhood witnesses this expulsion, they realize that something serious had happened.

Jeremiah

Jeremiah 46–51 was a call concerning the surrounding kingdoms that God was still judge. Even if the bride of Yahweh had turned a deaf ear to the relationship, God would not allow the other nations to do the same. They would be judged for their injustices as well. Babylon would punish the mighty Egyptian power, where God's people were attempting to hide (Jeremiah 46). Babylon would punish Philistia, Moab, Amon, Edom, Syria, Kedar, Hazor, and Elam (Jeremiah 47–49). Nebuchadnezzar would be ruthless, but would show the world, including Israel, that Yahweh would not be dishonored. Those nations who had affairs with God's spouse would suffer as well. Such nations included Babylon, whom God would finally punish for being too brutal on the Jews (Jeremiah 50–51).

The book of Jeremiah ends with the story of the punishment of Jerusalem (Jeremiah 52). Yahweh was a God of honor, and those who abuse the Creator of the world and the children will suffer—and especially those who are bound by a relationship to their Lord. The message was clear: in order for God to be fair and just, those in relationship with Yahweh must be treated the same as those outside the covenant. The children of Yahweh have no right to judge those outside the family, especially if they do not love and honor their spouse.

I have often heard men and women judge their neighbors, friends, or those in public who are unfaithful to their spouses. I have heard preachers condemn from the pulpit "the heathen," who experience sexual infidelity, abuse, or sexual addictions. I have heard Christian leaders judge our political leaders for their loose ethics. Our public schools are resisted because they "teach bad things." Unfortunately the Christian community has not been the example we should be. I know many Christian leaders who are guilty of public sin and yet who encourage staff and other leaders to look away. Some parents model dysfunctional marriages and teach their children that relationships are not meant to be healthy. Repentance becomes cheap and forgiveness forced. Our communities reject the church because they see an unfaithful spouse who justifies sin. While the neighbors watched as God "kicked out" the unfaithful spouse, Jeremiah reminded them that "adultery" is unacceptable for anyone.

Many of those who point the finger are themselves guilty of infidelity. It is easier to beat up on others rather than to confront ourselves. It is easier to hide the sins of those we know and love while openly castigating those who do the same sins in public. It is easier to ask God to send us as prophets to Moab rather than to our home city of Jerusalem. Jeremiah's book ends with the reminder that God does not tolerate a dysfunctional relationship and will not be abused. If God is to be known and glorified in the world, it must begin with those in covenant. God seeks relationship but it is a relationship of love, trust, respect, and honor.

Jeremiah and Modern Advocates

Yahweh seeks relationships, but they are to be healthy relationships. God deserves to be honored and loved in relationship with the creation. In Genesis 1 the creation responded obediently to Yahweh's word. The same should be true of humans. While God acknowledged that humans would desire evil from childhood (Gen 8:21), God still initiated a covenant with the human race. In Jeremiah God decided to confront the nation for breaking faith, unfaithfulness, and oppressing their own people. As any hurt spouse Yahweh expressed anger, grief, frustration, and a sense of betrayal. Even though God offered hope of change and a new relationship, Judah refused to repent. Yet Yahweh still initiated relationship as a renewed covenant that they could keep. Yahweh hoped against all hope and put faith in a people who "might" change their ways.

Jeremiah was God's advocate who empathized with Yahweh's suffering and also represented the unfaithful nation. If we imagine Jeremiah as a psychotherapist, then he was called to bring the two parties (Judah and Yahweh) together and attempt to work through the pain his client (Yahweh) expressed. For Jeremiah, these sessions were painful. He expressed fear, frustration, anger, and grief. He, like his God, was traumatized by, on the one hand, the denial and neglect of a nation and, on the other hand, the raw emotion and anger of a victim. At times he could not contain his shared suffering and anger, and confronted his people for their abuse and insensitivity. Yet through the sessions, he realized that Yahweh was still willing to hold out hope of change and offer of forgiveness.

Jeremiah was able to share the vision of what could be, which touched his own life even in sleep. Jeremiah was the counselor who could not leave this session at the office, but who allowed it to transform his experiences. Jeremiah was not a crazy spokesman for God, he was a traumatized therapist who some would say, "became too wrapped up in his work."

Over the years I have presented at biblical scholars' conferences concerning domestic abuse and the faith community. Often members of the group want to ask how I reconcile a loving God with the God of the prophets who is controlling, abusive, and oppressive to the nation of

Israel. They suggest that this may give batterers, stalkers, and oppressive males the scriptural backing to control others. I believe that the text suggests that God is passionate, and is hurt by the people of Israel. Batterers and controlling males are narcissistic and oppress females and vulnerable others because they are insecure. They stalk and control others because they need to increase control. Usually they are the ones bringing pain to their partners, and the victims have "no choice" in their daily lives. Contrast this with a God who allows the covenant partner free will, choice, and even forgiveness. God truly provides blessings to God's people—so much that adulterous Judah could not find fault with Yahweh.

The first thing to note is that Yahweh was reacting out of anger, hurt, and suffering because *Yahweh is the oppressed partner.* Second, *Yahweh was venting because of this hurt.* While the language is graphic, it does not always suggest that God will literally punish Israel. Third, *metaphorical language expresses hurt in God rather than prescribes divine punishment.* Finally, even though Yahweh claimed responsibility for the suffering and destruction of Israel and Judah, God did not directly punish. Babylon, Assyria, and other kingdoms *were allowed* to enter the cities to destroy them. The Hebrew Bible describes Yahweh as the divine hero who holds back evil forces, nature, and the enemy. God is protector. However, when God's spouse committed adultery Yahweh eventually stopped protecting and providing for the unfaithful partner. Israel was acting as an abuser, not Yahweh.

Traumatized Counselors, Ministers, or Prophets Today

Jeremiah challenges God's people to become involved in the lives of others. For the minister the struggle to "leave it at the office" is always present. Lori and I have always viewed this work as a team effort. When we planted a new church, some of the women requested that she become our Women's Minister. She quickly raised her own support and became financially compensated for the work she had always done. While I was thrilled to see her validated in this way, I have come to understand that keeping a paid position makes it more difficult for us to avoid taking our work to the coffee shop on our days off. We realize that ministry is who we are and that we will always have a shared passion for people.

The challenge is not leaving it at the office. The challenge that those in the faith community have is engaging our communities. Too often people

PART TWO   Advocates for Hope

try to separate themselves from their communities and expect their relationship with God to suffice in the spiritual life. However, Jeremiah challenges us to become advocates in our communities and for our God.

First, as advocates *we must become personally involved with our neighbors, our city, and our vocational communities.* Jeremiah experienced what God had seen and was there to engage people where they met, and community leaders where they lived. Second, *we also hope for change and bring a vision of what could be.* Many in our community struggle with guilt, shame, grief, abuse, and other forms of pain. Some self-medicate while others become oppressors. God's prophets are called to reframe their worldviews and paint a picture of a new hope, a different world, and an alternate reality. Third, just as Jeremiah confronted the corrupt political and religious leaders of his city, so *we may have to confront the comfort levels of our own Christian communities.* Finally, being involved means that *we carry a passion for God as well as a passion for people.* Spiritual and faith development mean that we seek a personal encounter with God as well as an encounter with our community. Many times I have our ministers and Agape members meet at Pioneer Courthouse Square to take to lunch and have a conversation those living on the streets. After that we meet at the square, read a Scripture together, and then discuss how our lunch conversation and experience applies to the text. Engaging the text calls us to do more than encounter God. It calls us to represent God in a world created in Yahweh's image. As Jeremiah was transformed while working with God and humans, so we experience this spiritual growth.

As advocates we must provide God's vision of hope for our community. God dreams of what could be and offers hope for change and transformation. I do believe that abusers, pimps, racists, sex offenders, and other oppressors can change. However, we still must provide safe environments for victims and potential victims by confronting oppression and holding them accountable. This can be overwhelming at times, as Jeremiah tells us, but it is the work we have been called to do.

The world will never understand God's vision of what could be unless we meet them where they are and tell them what plans God has for them.

5

Obadiah

Compassion and Empathy in God's House

A Need for Compassion and Empathy

ONE NIGHT I RECEIVED a call from Louie. Louie was one of the council members at Dignity Village. We met him one day when we did our first work project at the village. He had become homeless after growing addicted to heroin and alcohol and losing his family. He moved to Portland and was accepted into the Dignity Village community. After years of being clean and sober, he had become a respected leader at the village. He had been given the task to communicate with me in our work projects.

After one project Louie wanted to come to Agape to thank us on behalf of the village.

"I probably won't come back so don't get disappointed if I don't return to church. But I want to come this week to tell everyone thanks," he told me.

Louie came, thanked us, and rarely missed a Sunday church service for years. He helped lead our recovery ministry and benevolence work. He also became a bridge between Agape and Dignity Village and until his

PART TWO   Advocates for Hope

leaving and moving into a permanent residence, was one of our contacts in that community.

But back to the night of Louie's phone call. He had called me that night because one of the women of the Dignity Village community had cut herself repeatedly to the point that he was scared. He called an ambulance, which upset the woman, and asked me to come talk to the residents of the Village the next day. We talked about cutting (a form of self-injury) and why people sometimes hurt themselves in this way. Many who have experienced trauma or abandonment find that self-injury releases inner pain. Inner pain is hard to manage, but outer hurt can easily be controlled.

"We have a problem," Louie told me that night. "One of our first rules of the community is 'No harm to yourself or others.'" The village had adopted a list of rules that people needed to follow. Breaking one of these rules meant expulsion for a period of time. The council would take the matter to the residents, get their opinion, and make the decision. It was an attempt at democracy but one that typically did not exist on the streets. In this community, people were expected to follow a few basic rules and answer to their elected leadership. According to the first rule, the woman who had injured herself had to be "eighty-sixed" for a month. "I don't think that will help her or us, but rules are rules," Louie said. He was obviously worried about the woman and what would happen to her. However, the council felt the need to be fair and just.

The next day we all met and talked about her injury, fears of abandonment, and issues with her mom. A volatile conversation with her mother had triggered a fear that led to her cutting herself multiple times. The woman shared her story and the session with a counselor while we asked questions concerning her anxiety and issues that she faced. Louie and a few of the council leaders listened and offered examples of people they knew who had done the same. Council members also reinforced to the self-injurer that everyone was worried about her and were alarmed at what had happened. She seemed to feel safe and accepted in the community.

Afterward Louie and I talked. "Last night I was thinking and talking with some of the people about this first rule. She may have broken a rule, but it doesn't fit here," he said. "We think it might be good to bend the rule in this case."

I smiled. "Yes, Louie, since her fear of abandonment seemed to trigger what happened, abandoning her may make this worse." I smiled again, "Yes, I think you all are right—that's what grace must be."

Obadiah

Bending the Rules with Compassion

Obadiah was a prophet called by God to preach concerning the fall of the kingdom of Edom. Edom/Esau was the brother of Jacob, the father of the people of Israel, whose twelve sons became the tribes of Israel. It is hard to determine if Obadiah preached to the people of Edom directly or to the Judeans concerning their Edomite relatives.

Edom was located on the southern borders of Judah and Reuben (south of the Dead Sea). The nation of Moab separated Edom from Reuben, but Edom was known for harassing Israel, his brother. Edom was located where Arabia exits today.

When Jerusalem was sacked by the Babylonians, Edom evidently joined the Babylonians in the punishment.

> Because of the violence against your brother Jacob, you will be covered with shame and destroyed forever. On the day you stood in opposition while strangers carried off his wealth and foreigners entered his gates and cast lots for Jerusalem, you were like one of them. You should not watch your brother in the day he was cut down, nor rejoice over the people of Judah in the day of their destruction, nor boast in the day of their trouble. You should not march through the gates of my people in the day of their disaster, nor watch them in their misfortune nor seize their wealth in the day of their disaster. You should not stand at the crossroads to cut down their escapees, nor hand over their survivors in the day of their trouble. (Obad 8–14)

Brothers often stand together when their family is threatened. However, in this case Edom turned on his brother Jerusalem, helped the enemy, laughed at Jerusalem's misfortune, and cleaned up the leftovers. Edom (also called Easu) was known as a godless brother who sold his birthright for a bowl of stew (Gen 25:29–34). The people of Edom lived up to the reputation of Esau, Jacob's brother, by devouring God's chosen. While God had sent the Babylonians to punish Israel, Edom was not expected to "jump on the dog pile." Even worse, Edom refused to show mercy to Judah—unlike the Babylonians, who left survivors to repopulate the city.

God's judgment of Edom was simple. "The day of Yahweh is near for all nations/gentiles. As you have done, it will be done to you; your actions will return upon your own head" (Obad 15). Edom was also punished. After Babylon crushed Jerusalem, they would turn on their next victim. This too was God's judgment (Obad 1–7). Even though Israel would return and rebuilt its city, Edom would not recover: "But on Mount Zion will be deliverance; it will be holy, and Jacob will possess his possessions. Jacob will be a fire and Joseph a flame; Esau will be kindling and they will ignite and be destroyed. Esau, there will be no survivors. Yahweh has spoken . . . The kingdom will be Yahweh's" (17–21). The people of Edom watched their brother Jacob suffer, so God would make sure Edom would be crushed. The prophet preached a message of doom and it was well deserved. The Edomites were a people who had the chance to act with compassion, but they chose a different direction. Therefore they suffered as they had caused others to suffer. They failed to express compassion.

Why Compassion?

Compassion is a choice. While not everyone believes this, we at Agape Church of Christ have found that people can choose the way of compassion over the way of punishment.

Some refuse to practice compassion because they were abused. Those who are raised in abusive families can choose compassion as adults, or they can choose to repeat the cycle of punishment, violence, abuse, pain, and or suffering. Some choose to abuse others just as they were abused: "I was abused so I will abuse you," they say. Their children suffer. Their partners suffer. Their dependent elderly parents suffer. Their friends suffer. They bully because they were bullied. They are mean because they were demeaned. They inflict because they were afflicted. Their philosophy often is, my life was hell, so I'll make sure your life is a living hell as well. They hurt first before they are hurt. They refuse to act with compassion toward others.

Some neglect others because they themselves were abused. These have avoided feeling pain or have pretended it was not there. Unfortunately they become numb and emotionally ignore those with whom they are in relationship. Their philosophy is, it could be worse; you could have been treated like I was. Those who need love, compassion, grace, forgiveness, nurturing, and acceptance from these former sufferers of abuse are kept at an emotional distance. The new victims suffer silently and wonder what they did wrong: how can he or she be so distant from us? Neglect can be more damaging than physical abuse. They too withhold compassion.

Still others neglect themselves because they were abused. They work extremely hard in their jobs, chores, tasks, and volunteer service. They find identity in success and overwork. However, they will never be happy because they choose to neglect themselves. No one will fill that need they have for acceptance unless they learn to accept themselves. They avoid conflict and neglect the little prophet God placed within them that cries out for justice. They are not insensitive but are neglecting their own life. They cannot love their neighbor because they do not love themselves. They resist compassion.

Yet others abuse themselves because they suffered. These truly believe they deserved to be punished, or they feel ashamed of their past. They don't want or intend to hurt their relatives, but they do. Those who love these self-abusers agonize over why they sabotage personal success and satisfaction. The philosophy of these self-abusers is, I was abused, therefore I abuse myself. I was weak, I was vulnerable, I am ashamed. Therefore I'm unworthy of anything good. They resent compassion.

Because we have been hurt, we continue to injure others as well as ourselves. It is a vicious cycle. However, cycles are meant to be broken. Empathy is the ability to feel what another person feels. Usually when one person shares with us feelings, emotions, and thoughts, empathy causes us to feel what the other person feels. This is similar to sympathy, which is the ability to agree with what another person feels or to attempt to alleviate another person's suffering.[1] However, empathy is much stronger than sympathy, because it allows one to identify and connect emotionally with another person. When people share their stories with me that involve trauma, struggle, pain, fear, or suffering, empathy helps me to hurt for them, to emotionally connect with them, and to understand what they feel and are needing to share. Empathy is an act of becoming vulnerable with another person's humiliation and feeling their pain. Empathy provides me with a logical and emotional reason not to victimize others.

Compassion, however, consists of the emotions one feels that allow for empathy. Usually when I hear the stories from people who suffer, I become affected (this is a type of trauma) and emotionally moved to hurt for another. Compassion is the emotion that causes me to feel and have empathy. Compassion and empathy work together to help an individual feel another's pain and to act mercifully toward others. Empathy is also thought to help individuals in their development of personal and moral ethics. Empathic arousal happens as a child develops compassion by maturing in five steps:[2]

---

1. Thomas, *Moral Development Theory*, 157.
2. Ibid., 156–58.

- I cry because I hear someone else crying.
- I cry because their crying reminds me of a bad moment in my life.
- I cry because I want to cry with them.
- We cry together as a way to communicate.
- I am able to put myself in their place and cry along with them.

Empathy develops as a child matures and accepts the pain of others. However, the final two bullet points above are not automatic responses and require the individual to reflect on his or her experiences as they relate to the lives of others. In other words, adolescents or young adults develop empathy when they begin to think of others before themselves.

This is why empathy is an important moral virtue. Empathy helps the young boy continue to reciprocate in community and identify with those suffering in our society.

Empathy, Compassion, and Transformation

The kingdom of God's power has always been displayed by the ability to liberate people from oppression and from being oppressors. God's empire was expected to focus on social justice, to identify with the marginalized, and to lead the way in justice, healing, and freedom for many vulnerable people. Even though Christian history has been infected with the Crusades, ethnic cleansing, abuses, political control, and other sinful acts, the church worldwide has mainly focused on freeing the oppressed. In this ministry the church has identified with the mission of Jesus, who came to free the oppressed and seek and save those who were perishing (Luke 4:16–19; 19:11). In reaching the humiliated, God's people have identified with and helped them through compassion, empathy, mercy, and love.

It is this empathy and compassion that have empowered those living under the reign of God to practice love and accept all people. My family and I, our church, and many other people in Portland occasionally join Marshall and Leslie Snyder of Bridgetown Ministries in their Nightstrike ministry. Nightstrike began in 2002 with Marshall and Leslie's taking a pan of water under one of Portland's many bridges and washing the feet of those who were homeless. They would clean their feet, give them a new pair of socks and, in their words, "love the people of Portland." Over time people joined this weekly event to give haircuts, food, blankets, sleeping bags, clothing, prayers, and conversation to over two hundred people who come weekly to be loved by the many Portlanders who are there.

What began with a vision and decision to love has grown into a ministry embraced by Portland's vulnerable people and political leaders, who appreciate what this Bridgetown Church's ministry, members, and teens do for the community. When we come to serve, we hear people say, "This is what Christianity is all about." While our Christian history may sometimes suggest otherwise, our vision is to love and embrace people who need it most. Empathy and compassion are key components in the social, intellectual, and spiritual development of all people. These virtues also come forth in the ability of people to give back (reciprocate) to others.

God asks us to manifest the qualities of our Creator. Yahweh upholds justice, love, faithfulness, mercy, compassion, and grace. If we are to reflect God's nature, then we should manifest those qualities—because they are who God is. If we have been hurt or neglected, it sometimes seems logical to hurt or neglect others. However, nothing good can come of hurting as we have been hurt. In fact, we know this to be true. It was not good for us; therefore it can't be good for others. Someone needs to break the cycle, the rules, and the village contract. Grace causes us to act differently. Grace and compassion help us to rise above the endless cycles of pain and defense and to intervene with peace. The prophet Obadiah reminds us that God expects compassion from others.

The church is faced with a dilemma: We live in a nation that values rights, justice, truth, and equality (or at least we tell people we live in this type of nation). We sometimes become angry because some people in our country receive free health care, supplemental income, food stamps, and other benefits while we work hard so that we can pay to have these blessings. These are the blessings of living in a free country. These are the blessings of being in a country where the working class pays taxes. Unfortunately, these do not seem like blessings for us when we have to pay large sums of money to have them, while others receive them free. Instead of being happy that those who struggle to live can live with blessings, we complain and try to ignore them.

I have for years taken homeless people in Portland to lunch and asked if they were safe. I have at times eaten lunch with them on the sides of streets. The homeless are correct when they tell us that people criticize them, ignore them, or look at them with disgust. I have sat by their side when this happened. It is intimidating. It is embarrassing. It sometimes is a reminder of what I have done to them in the past.

I try to remind people that the issue is not about what is right, fair, or just. It is about compassion. What does compassion say to this issue?

PART TWO   Advocates for Hope

How do we as God's people respond out of mercy in these situations? If we are proud of ourselves and know that it's not about how much money we make but the fact that we have a job and can pay our taxes, then shouldn't we want the same for others?

When it comes to the current conversation about "illegal immigrants" in our country God's people are forced into the discussion. While I understand both sides of the arguments involving the affects of having people come to the United States without the proper documentation, I know that Obadiah calls us to ask the question, what does compassion say to the issue? Are we bringing this question to the table when we work in our community?

The family of my son's friend Mario had come from Mexico to this country. Most of the children in the family were born in the United States and so are automatically citizens. However, his mother and dad had stayed in Portland illegally. When my son's friend was in junior high, the factory where his parents worked was raided, and both were found to be here illegally. Because Margarita had children at home, she was allowed to stay. Her husband, however, was sent back to Mexico.

I understand why he was sent home. I know that many unemployed U.S. citizens cannot compete with the number of undocumented people who work cheaply and without insurance. I do believe that people should be in the United States legally and need to work with our government to obtain the proper visas and documents of citizenship. I spent many hours helping people in our church's English as Second Language (ESL) ministry prepare for their citizenship tests. We would bring the families forward at church to celebrate their passing the test and becoming U.S. citizens.

However, I wonder how creating a "fatherless" environment is helpful for a family—especially for my son's friend and others like him, who spend the most important years of maturation without a father. When Mario would come to our house, I would ask him if he had talked to his father. He did not see his father throughout his teen years. I thought about the many times I had gone to the Immigration and Naturalization Service office to advocate for those in this country who were in danger of being sent home. They had become valuable to us in translating, teaching, and conducting mission work abroad.

I found myself asking the question, how do grace and compassion fit into this situation?

I wonder what Obadiah would have said to us?

6

Habakkuk

Crying Out for Mercy

Struggling to Be Merciful

"Look Ed," I enunciated, showing my anger, "when we set an appointment, I expect you to be there. I am very busy and I don't like being stood up. I don't have to meet with you. Remember, you are the one charged with a crime; you are the one being punished. You are the one who has to change—not me. You got it?"

Ed was sitting across from me in the booth at a Shari's restaurant looking down at the table. He nodded slowly. Ed was in his early twenties and had three kids. His wife, Sarah, had just left him, and he had just been released from jail. He had assaulted his wife one night and ripped her shirt as he grabbed her. His statement was, "She was leaving the room, and I was trying to talk to her. I grabbed her to make her talk to me."

When Sarah came to me, the incident had happened barely an hour before. Lori and I had her go to the police, file the report, and take the kids to her parents. Abuse is wrong. We had a no-tolerance policy at our church when it came to domestic violence.

PART TWO   Advocates for Hope

The next day we went with Sarah to the courthouse, as she filed an order of protection (formerly called a restraining order). She bravely stood before the judge and the order was granted. Because Ed had assaulted his wife in the presence of their children, he was arrested and tried the next day.

Ed was mandated to two years in a batterer-intervention program. I had him contact a friend who ran an approved program and began the process of supporting him in his repentance. He could not come to our church because we chose to support his wife, but I agreed to work with him to find a different church in which to heal.

Ed sat across from me and looked at the table.

"I'm sorry I didn't show," he said.

Then he stared at the table. Tears formed in his eyes. "I—I don't know what to do. I have nothing. I don't know how this happened."

Suddenly I was not angry. I looked at Ed and saw the tears in his eyes. He was a kid. He and Sarah had married early and already had three boys. He didn't have a job. He was living apart from his boys. He had to move in with his parents, who had not provided a good model of responsibility for him. I remembered looking at the stack of papers delivered to him by the sheriff's deputy, which included the order of protection that he was served from Sarah. This restraining order I helped Sarah complete was already ten pages, but more pages were attached that explained his responsibility to the county court. Ed had brought the papers to our first meeting. The language of these documents was difficult for me to read, and so also for a young man who had barely finished high school. I remembered my conversation with Stacey Womack, the director of ARMS (Abuse Recovery Ministry and Services). We both agreed that Ed was young, at an early enough stage to change, but had a lot to overcome to stay healthy.

I'm not making excuses for Ed's abusive behavior. But that first moment at Shari's restaurant was a moment in mercy for me. I had two choices: continue to verbally abuse him for disappointing me, or forgive him and move on. The first option was bothering me, and I was tired of being angry. The second option was the right choice, and I had been resisting that for the past week.

"It's okay, Ed," I said. "Let's just move on and start working with Stacey in your counseling."

Ed needed an advocate. He needed me as his minister to stand before God and pray for him. Sarah had support from Jesus, Lori, her survivors support group, and our church. Ed had a group of guys who had been abusive, a female facilitator, his parents, and me. I believe that he had Jesus, who reached out to him through his group, program, and legal system. But Ed needed a prophet who would advocate before the good judge of the world. I had to decide at that table if I would be that prophet.

Cleaving to Mercy

Habakkuk was a prophet during the reign of Jehoiakim in Judah. The book doesn't give us a setting, tell us any more of who Habakkuk was, or share any background. It simply begins by stating that it is an oracle given to Habakkuk the prophet. The name *Habakkuk* means "a garden plant," "to clasp," or to "comprehend/hold closely."[1] It is clear that he was an advocate for the city of Jerusalem. The mention of God leading the Chaldeans (another term for Babylonians) in Hab 1:6 suggests that he experienced God's punishment on Jerusalem. In 604 BCE. King Nebuchadnezzar attacked the Philistines on the coast of Palestine and then advanced toward Jerusalem. Habakkuk's vision seems like a vision of a storm cloud from the coast invading the small city of Jerusalem.

Habakkuk complains about the violence that the city experienced. The prophet claims that God did not hear his cries for help and that his people's punishment was extreme: "How long, Yahweh, will I cry for help, but you do not listen? I shout to you, 'Violence!' but you do not save. Why do you make me look at injustice? Why do you tolerate wrong? Destruction and violence are present; there is tension, and conflict increases. Therefore the law is paralyzed, and justice doesn't win. The wicked controls the righteous, so that justice is corrupted" (1:2–4). While the people of Judah were punished for corruption, Habakkuk felt that this punishment from God was excessive. According to the prophet, the bloodshed, violence, and captivity did not bring "justice" but further suffering.

God's response in Hab 1:5–11 is to send this powerful (police) force of Babylon to judge the world and kill the disobedient. These who would come were ruthless, impetuous, predatory, violent, self-confident, and mechanically advanced. They carried out their own form of justice (1:6–10). According to Habakkuk, this empire was not interested in fulfilling Yahweh's justice; they were hired mercenaries who would punish

---

1. Redditt, *Introduction to the Prophets*, 300; Roberts, *Nahum, Habakkuk, and Zephaniah*, 86; and Szeles, *Habakkuk and Zephaniah*, 4.

as they pleased. To the prophet this was not justice; it was cruel and unusual punishment.

Habakkuk further questioned and confronted God. Was this just? Was this fair? For the prophet, the eternal God, who could not tolerate evil, was uncharacteristically silent during this "cruel and unusual punishment." While Habakkuk did not deny that Jerusalem had sinned, he was not afraid to challenge Yahweh concerning their punishment. How could a holy and loving God stand by while an army of ruthless thugs slaughtered the chosen people? "You, Yahweh, have appointed them to execute judgment; you, my rock, have ordained them to punish. Your eyes are too pure to look on evil and you cannot observe wrongdoing. Why then do you observe the unrighteousness? Why are you idle while the wicked swallow up those more righteous than they?" (1:12-13)

The prophet's concern was for his people. Yahweh had allowed a wicked army to punish the Jewish nation, yet Habakkuk wondered at what point they would be stopped and sent home. When will this army of thugs finish their task, and how far will they go to destroy the Jews? Could there be justice in this brutal penal system? Even more Habakkuk confidently took a stand to hear Yahweh's answer. "I will stand at my watch and station myself at the post; I will look to see what God will say to me, and how I will answer this complaint" (Hab. 2:1). The prophet was not only an advocate for the guilty; he questioned the eternal Creator of the universe concerning the appointed and approved judgment. Just as Abraham bargained with God over the destruction of Sodom and Gomorrah (Gen 18:22–33), Habakkuk questioned Yahweh's motives and method of judgment.

The straightforward statement in Hab 2:2 ("Then Yahweh replied/answered,") suggests that Yahweh responded to Habakkuk's challenge: "Then Yahweh replied/answered: 'Write down the revelation and make it clear on the tablets so that a messenger may run with it,'" (2:2). God told the prophet to record what would occur in Judah's future. Yahweh listed the crimes of the chosen people because they demanded justice. They were arrogant (2:5), were greedy, practiced extortion (2:6), murdered the innocent, acted unjustly, enticed others to addictions (2:15), and worshiped other gods (2:18–19). Many of the sins were committed by the upper class and by leaders of the community. The kingdom of Judah had sinned and flagrantly violated their covenant with God. Not only had they abandoned the one true God by worshiping idols, but they had oppressed their own people. While the punishment seemed extreme to Habakkuk, Yahweh was clear: "you will be treated as you treated others." What Obadiah and Jeremiah had spoken in their prophecies, so Habakkuk also spoke: the oppressor would become the victim. The bully would be bullied.

Yet in the midst of this legal letter that is the book of Habakkuk, a letter e-mailed (so to speak) throughout the land, Yahweh reminded Habakkuk and the readers that the survivors would live. First, *those who were faithful would survive*. "See, the enemy is puffed up; his desires are not honest—but the righteous person will live by their faithfulness" (2:4). The Hebrew world usually translated "faith" is *chesed*. This word refers to faithfulness (dependability) in a covenant relationship. For Yahweh those who stayed faithful would endure the violence. Faithfulness is extolled not only in Habakkuk but also in other prophetic books. Therefore in the book of Daniel, facing Nebuchadnezzar's fiery furnace, Shadrach, Meshach, and Abednego prove faithful to God while in Babylon (Daniel 3). For Isaiah, *chesed* involved waiting (Isa 40:31) Isaiah does not promise that the faithful will not suffer during Judah's judgment. He issues a call to those enduring punishment to stay committed to Yahweh. God still looks for people to be faithful to the covenant. The time of punishment is not the end of the relationship. It is a call to return to Yahweh and commit to obedience.

A second glimmer of hope that God offered Habakkuk was that *in punishment Yahweh was glorified*. "Has not Yahweh Almighty determined that the people's labor is only fuel for the fire, that the nations exhaust themselves for nothing? For the earth will be filled with the knowledge of the glory of Yahweh as the waters cover the sea" (2:13–14). All kingdoms would see God's hand and understand that Yahweh required obedience. A common theme in the prophets is that God seeks to be known in relationship and in obedience. When Israel turned from Yahweh to idols, Yahweh was dishonored and shamed. God had to act in judgment of idol worship for the sake of honor and glory.

Many times I have told abusive men, dysfunctional families, and parents who have neglected their children that God seeks to be honored by their lives. If they cannot provide a safe environment for their children, partners, or spouses, then God will intervene to protect the vulnerable ones. I share that Jesus will use the police, the legal system, child-protective services, counselors, or other organizations to create a safe place for these victims. Finding safety may include punishing oppressors. God does this to be honored. God is the defender of the oppressed. Jesus was the friend of sinners and tax collectors. Therefore we must honor God by also providing a healthy environment for those who trust us. We also glorify God when the vulnerable ones of our world are protected and safe.

Church leaders who do not protect children, confront pedophiles, and report abusive individuals, who do not oppose racism, create a safe environment for vulnerable people, or treat other members and their community with respect will experience a Babylonian invasion. God expects to be honored and glorified in our communities, just as God had expected to be honored and glorified in the communities of biblical Israel and Judah. In the midst of suffering God is to be honored in the city. The church should not be the reason God enacts judgment. The church should be a place that extends God's justice and outreach into the community. Sometimes a church's door closes permanently because God needs to be honored in the city.

Finally, *in the midst of punishment, Yahweh was present*. For the prophet Yahweh was present in the temple during the people's injustice and their suffering. "Yahweh is in the holy temple; let all the earth be silent/quiet" (2:20). While some may have thought that God had abandoned them, they were wrong. Their God was with them through the suffering and injustice that they experienced. While it seemed that Yahweh had also abandoned the victims of the Babylonian invasions, the temple was still occupied by the Lord of the universe. Whether or not God acted was not the point. Yahweh was there, and all the earth was to be quiet.

The Other Side of Mercy

One of the most difficult parts of our ministry has been to explain that Jesus is present during times of suffering and injustice. The crucifixion of Jesus, the destruction of Yahweh's temple (twice), and the injustice of a people who claimed to follow their God are examples of God's presence in and during oppression and humiliation. God was present when David offered sacrifices and while he concealed the sin against Bathsheba and Uriah. God was present during Manasseh's reign of terror. God was present during Jehoshaphat's, Hezekiah's, and Josiah's reforms of their kingdom. God was present when Babylon cut down men, women, and children and destroyed the temple. God was present when Daniel, Shadrach, Meshach, and Abednego were thrown into the fire and the lions' den (Daniel 3; 6).

Habakkuk

God was present when Jesus felt abandoned and cried out, "My God, my God, why have you forsaken me?" (Mark 15:34). Jesus suffers with those who suffer, and in the cross (and many other places in the Bible) God identifies with those who suffer. God is present today in our suffering—whether from cancer, abuse, genocide, oppression, sickness, murder, despair, grief, rejection, loss, or humiliation. Whether we suffer or not, Yahweh is present in the temple of our body and community; therefore all should be respectful.

The book of Habakkuk ends with a prayer from the prophet. Chapter 3 is distinct from the first two chapters. It is labeled a prayer with a singing instrument and takes the form of an ancient psalm. After he confronts Yahweh in chapters 1 and 2, Habakkuk writes a song to his Lord. The prophet's courage had been displayed by his willingness and desire to confront Yahweh for Jerusalem's impending judgment. Yet after the prophet had seen the vision of what would happen and realized that Babylon would do to Jerusalem what they had to other nations and people, he wrote a song or prayer for the city. The song features common language for theophanies (manifestations of God) and describes the Day of Yahweh as one of the ancient Israelite battles where God defeated the people's enemies.[2] "Yahweh, I have heard of your fame; I stand in awe of your deeds, Yahweh. Repeat them in our day, in our time make them known; in wrath remember mercy" (Hab 3:2). The prophet knew that God must be glorified and honored.

He knew Yahweh's reputation was at stake. Yet he asked for mercy and renewal. Habakkuk 3:3–15 was written in apocalyptic style. Apocalyptic was an ancient Near Eastern genre. Metaphors, images, symbols, and exaggerations create a story and captivate the reader or hearer. In apocalyptic the gods were roused out of the heavens to come to the earth and deal with the enemy. In this section of Habakkuk, Yahweh marches into Jerusalem and fights evil. While in reality it was the Babylonians who came to the city, Yahweh was responsible for (the author of) this judgment. It must have been a horrible scene to witness (2:6).

How horrible it must have been for the prophet to know that the author of Jerusalem's life was the one who took it away. The scene was so disturbing that Habakkuk was traumatized. As when one experiences a bad LSD trip or traumatic flashback, so here Habakkuk can only stand, watch, and hold on for his life. His only hope was that God would turn

---

2. Hiebert, *The God of My Victory*, 138–39.

PART TWO   Advocates for Hope

to mercy and, in the end, punish Babylon for their lack of compassion (Hab 2:6).

Habakkuk chose to rejoice during this time. While it would have seemed odd to believe that Habakkuk would have been smiling and cheering the Babylonians on, the point was that his calling was to endure and believe in God. Even in punishment hope must exist, and the prophet had to bring that hope. Even in punishment one must know that they can turn to God and receive grace and forgiveness.

The Other Response in Mercy

At the start of this chapter, I told the story of Ed. Over the years I have had many Eds. I have tried to walk the road with men who have lost what is precious to them through their own poor choices, dysfunctions, and woundedness. Numerous counselors, advocates, attorneys, probation and parole officers, therapists, coaches, teachers, ministers have advocated for people trying to get their lives in order. Many ask us why God is causing the suffering. Some suggest that the abusers are the real victims. Some suggest that the system is unfair. Some people give up and give in. All, however, need hope and someone who can offer a clear picture of the bigger issue.

As a follower of God, I believe that the hope we offer is not a quick-fix remedy. It is not a magical feel-good pep talk. It must be a real acceptance of responsibility and wrongdoing, and a desire to make amends (we call this repentance). First, *it must be a willingness on the part of an abuser to change, stop the sinful behavior, and validate the true victims.* It is not important whether the punishment of abusers is fair. It is imperative that we become faithful, trustworthy, honest, and just. This must be what we decide for God; then we promise to be faithful to our community, families, and selves.

Second, *it is important for an abuser to ask, how was God glorified by my actions?* This is difficult. To admit that hitting one's spouse; calling the children worthless; labeling sons girls and daughters sluts; using emotional abuse; disengaging from core relationships through drugs, alcohol, pornography, gambling, or other addictions—to admit that these behaviors shame God (or Jesus) is difficult, but it is honest. Jesus acts to bring glory to God, and no matter how painful our actions, God is to be glorified. Telling others that God had to confront us to bring glory to the

Holy One is humbling but healing. Affirming that God speaks out for the powerless also affirms God's justice and care for victims in our society.

Finally, *during justice Yahweh is present*. I believe that Jesus is present during suffering and oppression for the victims and for the oppressor. This does not mean that being in the presence of the oppressor is the same as standing with the oppressor. God opposes oppression but is present to confront and challenge. Oppressors are to be silent in Yahweh's presence.

The Modern Song of the Prophet

Since I converted to Christianity, I have been exposed to a new *F* word for twenty-nine years. It is hard to believe, but that *F* word (*forgive, forgiveness*) has had a tremendous impact on how we see oppressors. We are taught that we are to forgive when someone does something bad to us. We are taught that it is wrong to hope for them to be punished. When a bully is taken out, we don't know whether to cheer or put on a sad face. We are taught that "pride goes before a fall," so we shouldn't be happy when a pedophile receives "jailhouse justice" while in prison. We are taught that forgiveness is expected of us, even though our spouse or partner physically abuses us and then asks for forgiveness. Many times forgiveness is demanded and we oblige them by giving it.

Countless women have approached me after my presentations about domestic and sexual abuse, misogyny, and the response of faith communities. These women are Jewish, Christian, Muslim, Baha'i, or from other faiths. They tell me that their faith community did not support them in leaving their husband—no matter whether he was abusive, addicted to pornography, or continually in other sexual relationships during their marriage. Clergy would tell these women that they had the responsibility to forgive since the man had confessed his sin before the faith community. In many cases clergy confronted the victim but not the abuser, sex addict, or adulterer. These women share with me what it is like to live with these men and see the hypocrisy that they displayed at church and then in their home. The victims relate how "dirty" they feel when their husbands touched them or when they caught them viewing pornography or thinking about abusive behavior. Women have confessed to me how angry they are because they feel like prisoners while their husbands (as well as church leaders) continue to control them. Many explain to me that they not only have had to leave their spouse, but they feel they had to leave their faith community by divorcing their spouse. In their minds, God was oppressive. However, after hearing our presentations on abuse or on healthy marriages, these women share that they feel validated and realize that God confronts the colonizer, not the colonized. God calls for repentance first, then forgiveness. Jesus offers healing, but the offender rather than the victim must be confronted with justice.

I agree that we are called to forgive. Jesus tells us that if we can't forgive others their sins, we will not be forgiven (Matt 6:14–15). However, we are not taught that repentance, justice, and reconciliation are key ingredients to healing and forgiveness. Forgiveness typically is the last step toward reconciliation. Previously there must be validation of suffering by the offender, repentance, justice, and confession before the offended party can forgive. Even more, if the offender refuses to take any of the above steps, forgiveness and reconciliation cannot happen. The God of grace, love, and forgiveness models for us this form of reconciliation. Upon repentance God offers forgiveness. However, if the offender continues to be stubborn, rebellious, and in denial, forgiveness is not typically extended. Forgiveness is a choice, an offer of grace by the offended party when they are validated.

If the offender chooses not to stop their abusive behavior, justice must be served. We Americans live in a country with this form of justice. We do rejoice when a dangerous criminal is taken to jail. We do not rejoice because he suffers, but we rejoice for the victims and the future potential victims who have been spared.

Am I Willing to Be Habakkuk?

God appealed that I would walk with Ed and be faithful in his healing. Ed and I eventually parted ways because we had committed as a church to help his wife heal. This must have been difficult for him. (I don't know what happened to Ed. His wife left our church to join a church plant and healed in her life.) However, I do know that I learned a lot from Ed. I learned that emotionally beating up on the guy who did what many men have done—as well as on those of us who claim we would never hit our wives—is not the way of God. Habakkuk had the guts to stand up for others, and while some "got what they deserved," Yahweh needed a prophet to cry out, "Have mercy, Lord, and ease up while you are at it!"

Nancy Nason-Clark has done tremendous work in the faith community on domestic-violence prevention and batterer intervention. She has become not only a strong advocate in the faith community for victims, and she has cried out for mercy with batterers. She is confirming research that suggests that when a pastor is involved with a batterer who is in a state-approved intervention program, the batterer's chances of reoffending drop drastically.[3] Typically, few men who are abusive finish their court-mandated counseling. Many of the men who are abusive will reoffend. The research tells us that the more agencies that are involved in their intervention process, the more likely they are to stop being abusive. *There is hope.*

The church is not an abuse-prevention agency but has been viewed as a hindrance to addressing the problem of abuse in our communities. Fortunately Dr. Nason-Clark's research provides hope for churches and our communities. God's prophets can help our communities become safe places. However, it involves us walking with those who "get what they deserve" and crying out during their journey.

The research is clear . . . A prophet who cries for their people, no matter how guilty the people are, and holds them accountable will experience God's healing and mercy upon their community. It also suggests that advocating for others demands compassion, courage, and vision.

---

3. The Rave Project's most current research is available at: www.theraveproject.org.

7

Zephaniah

Voices in the Heart of the City

PIONEER COURTHOUSE SQUARE IS a favorite gathering place for many people in Portland. In *All God's Children*, by Rene Denfeld, it was described as a popular hangout for youth, street families, and the homeless who were spanging for money during the 1990s.[1] Drugs were commonly exchanged among many of the youth in the square. A Starbucks Coffee store sits at the top of the square while Pioneer Square Mall (a mall with very expensive stores) lies one block from the gathering place. Nordstrom's corporate offices loom above the square.

Battles have been fought over the square as well. Some of the wealthiest businesses in the United States (or those carrying the appearance of wealth) surround this small, brick-paved parcel of land located between two major light-rail lines. At one point the business leaders did not like looking down on a city landmark with people begging, smoking, loitering, exchanging drugs, and creating a disturbance. It was bad for business, the city, and the safety of the people. I have to agree on the one hand. So things changed.

Smoking was banned from the square. "No Sitting" and "No Camping" ordinances were enforced at the square and throughout the city.

---

1. Denfeld, *All God's Children*, 10–13.

Families were encouraged to come to the square. In the summers "Flicks on the Bricks" became a popular movie night at the square, and "Noon Toons" helped to fill the area during lunch. These events also seemed to provide a safe place to gather. This once "dark heart of the city" became a place where people felt safe and breathed fresh air once again. One thing remained constant.

First, the public restrooms at the TriMet ticket office *provided a safe and warm place for those in the city during the day*. Second, *Christian preachers and tract distributers continued to provide a word from God*. The message was that "God loves you, but . . . "

Typically we from Agape Church of Christ would come to the square and cross the light-rail tracks to the gathering, smoking, and "dirty people" on the "margins of the square of society." We would invite them to lunch, hug them, or talk with those we recognized. Ken Lloyd and his team from Home PDX Ministries would move among the group in the evenings to hand out sandwiches to those who were hungry. This ministry was asked to leave the square for a period of time, but the "Mall Police" asked that they be allowed back. "They do good work," was the reason the police officers gave for asking that they be allowed to help others.

While I am not opposed to the changes at this small tract of land, I have found it interesting how "public space" is viewed in cities. In Don Mitchell's book *The Right to the City*, he describes the public space of the city as a place of fear and anarchy.[2] Tragedies in major U.S. cities create a belief that the city is a place of darkness, chaos, and struggle. "Such an association of public space with anarchy is, of course, not new; it is not just a feature of the contemporary city, of the current media-encouraged, overwhelming concern about crime, homelessness, and random terrorism that makes public space seem such an undesirable attribute of the contemporary American city."[3] In the ancient world, however, the city was the place of safety reinforced by the surrounding walls, military protection, and the reminder that chaos and evil lay outside the walls of the city. Today the city seems to be a place of struggle and competition. The Occupy Wall Street movement has brought this to light by suggesting that the city is a place where all citizens can struggle for a voice and the right to speak.

---

2. "Public space engenders fears, fears that derive from the sense of public space as uncontrolled space, as a space in which civilization is exceptionally fragile" (Mitchell, *The Right to the City*, 13).

3. Ibid.

Yet who has the right to Pioneer Square? The surrounding businesses and wealthy mall, one block from the square, manifest competition more than the peaceful gathering of people. Even more, how is compassion (one of the major qualities of God) manifested in this public space? Further, how do God's prophets provide presence in this public space? Would the Hebrew prophets, for instance, preach a word of condemnation to those in the public gathering, or would they go to the mall or corporate offices and call for justice, compassion, and less greed? Would they verbally beat up those who seek refuge in the heart of the city, or would they challenge those who look out over the square and see "evil, darkness, or sin"?

Would God's prophets leave the safety of the "clean public space" to engage those driven out into a world of darkness, addiction, and painful memories?

God's Prophet to the City

Zephaniah began speaking during the reign of Josiah of Judah, as well as during the ministries of the prophets Jeremiah and Nahum. He would have spoken during turbulent times. Since he spoke against Assyria and Nineveh (which was destroyed 612 BCE), we can assume he preached between 630 and 614 BCE. His prophecy against surrounding Moab, Ammon, Libya (Cush), and Philistia suggests that the awesome "Day of Yahweh" would be a crisis that also affected people outside Jerusalem.

Zephaniah's judgment on Jerusalem may have referred to King Josiah's reforms (Zeph 1:2—2:3). Josiah eradicated idolatry and false worship in Judah. However, the distress mentioned also suggests that an army was coming to level the city rather than to purify a nation. The text does indicate that what would happen was a day of God's judgment.

The Day of the Lord

The common biblical metaphor for this divine event was "day of Yahweh," "the day," or "that time" (Zeph 1:7,8,9,10,14, 15,18; 2:2,3; 1:12; 2:2). The point of this language is that God has appointed a time/day to act, to pass judgment upon those guilty of sinning against their Lord. This notion of the Day of the Lord occurs often in the prophets to suggest God's anger, wrath, punishment, judgment, sacrifice, devastation, or "cutting off from the earth." The language was not literal. It does not predict an end of the planet, the end of the world, or the cessation of time. This symbolic language painted an oral picture of judgment for a listening audience. God was roused out of the heavens and came to the earth/Jerusalem to enact justice. Similar to a parent's yelling, "don't make me come up there," or, "do I need to stop this car?," the message communicated that Yahweh had tolerated enough and was going to act. "Yahweh ain't playin'!"

For those being oppressed, the Day of Yahweh was a day of justice, salvation, and freedom. For those who oppressed, this day was fearful.

> I will stretch out my hand against Judah and against all who dwell in Jerusalem. I will cut off the remnant of Baal worship from this place, the names of the idolatrous priests—those who bow down on the roofs to worship the hosts of heaven/sky, those who bow down and swear by Yahweh and who also swear by Molek, and those who turn back from following Yahweh and neither seek nor inquire of Yahweh.
>
> Be silent before Lord Yahweh, for the day of Yahweh is near. Yahweh has prepared a sacrifice; and sanctified those invited. "On the day of Yahweh's sacrifice I will punish the officials and the king's sons and all those wearing foreign clothes . . ." "On that day," declares Yahweh, 'a cry will go up from the Fish Gate, weeping from the New Quarter, and a loud crash from the hills."
> (1:4–10)

The Day of Judgment would be traumatic. As the armies Yahweh had sent entered the city, the guilty as well as the innocent would be punished. Those who continued to worship Baal, Molech, and the constellations would suffer (1:4–7). Political leaders who had turned from Yahweh (1:8) would be punished for their corruption. Those who chose not to act for justice (were complacent, 1:12) would also suffer. The day would be a violent display of justice upon a people that had rejected their God.

Whereas Habakkuk cries to Yahweh for mercy, Zephaniah seems to describe God's judgment in detail, almost as if he felt it were a good thing. The graphic depiction of violence indicates an abundance of grief and suffering on the pat of Jerusalemites. In light of this violent display of God's power in Zephaniah, Carol Dempsy asks if God's justice was fair: "The text seems to legitimate the use of destructive power for the sake of liberation in the face of oppression. While this may be understood as justice, is it really? And while power can have liberating effects, is there something further about power that needs to be grasped and executed if

PART TWO   Advocates for Hope

power is to be a truly liberating experience for all creation?"[4] Zephaniah describes in detail Jerusalem's sin, and justifies the punishment. Whereas Habakkuk was overwhelmed at the violence of the executioners, Zephaniah was overwhelmed at the sin of the unrighteous people of Judah.

While the punishment would be swift, brutal, and thorough, Zephaniah knew that some would need mercy. Zephaniah seems to be dwelling in the heart of the city, calling the people to gather for protection. "Gather yourselves together, shameful nation; the decree has not yet taken effect, and that day passes like windblown chaff. Yahweh's fierce anger has not yet come upon you, neither has the day of Yahweh's wrath. Seek Yahweh, all you humble of the land, and do what God commands. Seek righteousness, seek humility; perhaps you will be sheltered on the day of Yahweh's anger" (2:1–3) Notice the repeated call to unity.

Zephaniah's call that the people of Judah avoid Yahweh's wrath came as a call for repentance. This repentance was manifested by seeking Yahweh, righteousness, and humiliation. As a king calls people to bow and plead for mercy, so the prophet challenged those who feared Yahweh to unite and humble themselves. The Hebrew word meaning "humble" or "humiliated" is *ani*, which refers to poor, oppressed, vulnerable people. The prophet warns Jerusalem's residents that God's punishment is upon them; yet those who seek God and humble themselves have hope. Their hope was that Yahweh would show mercy.

In the ancient world the concept that today in English we call righteousness involved social justice. In Zephaniah's context, the rich, proud, and corrupt leaders of the city had oppressed the innocent, had failed to maintain devotion to Yahweh or to lead others in it, and had lived in excess. Yahweh called the people to become vulnerable and trust their God.

Zephaniah's Heart for People

Zephaniah was in the heart of the city gathering and calling the people to unite and seek safety. The prophet was not only among them. He eagerly desired to bring them to safety. They were all in this together. Zephaniah was not a preacher who simply "told it like it was," he begged people to join him and flee the punishment together.

The prophet then turns his attention to the other nations. If Yahweh did not allow the children of the covenant to get away with injustice, how

---

4. Dempsey. *The Prophets*, 144.

much more would those outside the family be held accountable! In this section of the book of Zephaniah, it doesn't matter to the prophet how severe the sins of the foreign kingdoms are; they were simply going to fall. Those pesky Philistines, who lived on the coast had been a perpetual thorn in Israel's side since the days of the judges and the first kings, would be punished. The Moabites and Ammonites, who surrounded the eastern side of Israel and the Dead Sea, would also suffer for insulting Yahweh's people (2:8–9). All three kingdoms would be destroyed (probably by Babylon) and their land inherited by the returning Judeans.

> Yahweh their God will care for them and will restore their fortunes. "I have heard the insults of Moab and the taunts of the Ammonites, who insulted my people and made threats against their land. Therefore, as I live," declares Yahweh Almighty, the God of Israel, Moab will become like Sodom, the Ammonites like Gomorrah—a place of weeds and salt pits, an eternal wasteland. The remnant of my people will loot them; the survivors of my nation will inherit their land." This is what they will receive in return for their pride, for insulting and mocking the people of Yahweh Almighty. (2:7–10)

The empires of Egypt (Cush) and Assyria would be completely destroyed (Nineveh fell in 612 BCE) by God's servant army and would suffer for their sins. "This is the city of rebellion that lived in security. She said to herself, 'I am the one! There is none besides me.' What a ruin she has become, a place for wild beasts! All who pass by her scoff and shake their fists" (2:15).

The doom of the Day of Yahweh was not limited to the city of Jerusalem but would affect the surrounding region as well. Yahweh, the God of all the earth, expected all the people to live under the reign of honor and justice.

The Day of Justice

If God expected justice from other peoples, how much more was justice expected from the chosen people of Israel! Jerusalem was guilty of oppressing people, disobeying God's law, rejecting and a relationship with Yahweh, and corruption in political and religious leadership. Jerusalem had rebelled against their God and turned away from their relationship with Yahweh. Yet God still tried to call the people of Judah to repentance.

First, *Yahweh reminds the people that they had a righteous God who dispensed justice within the city*. "Yahweh within her [i.e., the city] is righteous and does no wrong. Morning by morning justice is dispensed, and every new day God does not fall, yet the unrighteous do not know shame" (Zeph 3:5). While the people of Jerusalem were unjust, God continued to work among them and offer justice. God's honesty was not dependant upon their faithfulness.

Second, *God allows the kingdoms surrounding Jerusalem to be punished, in the hopes that they would also repent*. However, this did not drive Jerusalem or Judah to a full repentance initiative. The city was stubborn and would not turn their hearts to their God: "Of Jerusalem I thought, 'Now you will fear me and accept correction!' Then her place of safety would not be destroyed and all my punishments come upon her. But they were still eager to behave corruptly in all they did" (Zeph 3:7).

Finally, *Yahweh will allow the appointed armies to attack the city of Jerusalem in a last effort to turn them to their God*. "Therefore wait for me," declares Yahweh, 'for the day I will stand up to witness because I have decided to judge the nations/gentiles, to gather the kingdoms and to pour out my wrath on them—all my anger because the fire will burn up all the land. Then I will purify the lips of the peoples, that all of them may call on the name of Yahweh and serve together as one'" (3:8–9). God allows the city to fall and be punished because Yahweh hopes that they will change. It seems hard to understand that punishment would be used to help people respect their Lord. However, this is similar to the father who allows his son to go to jail and spend a few weeks experiencing prison life. Many things happen while the son is in prison, and as he is released, the father asks him what he learned in jail. Can the son blame his father for all that happened in prison? Can the son blame his father for leaving him in jail? Can the son accuse the father of being cruel and heartless? He may, but the experience sometimes reminds one that life is not safe and danger exists. The way to stay out of danger is to listen to and trust those who are teaching us a better way.

The Day After

The remainder of chapter 3 discusses God's blessings for those left behind in Jerusalem after the last deportation to Babylon. God will protect the meek, the humble, the lame, the oppressed, and immigrants from Judah to other areas. These people would be the "remnant" who would return to rebuild Judah. God's point is that after the punishment those in exile and those who survive in Jerusalem would be humbled by their experiences and would return to Yahweh and be dependent on God for their survival. Those who were arrogant would seem weak and mourn over their sin against God. This horrible "jailhouse" experience of being left behind in Jerusalem would change their lives and humble them before the mighty hand of their God.

> On that day you, Jerusalem, will be put to shame for all you have done to me, and I will remove your arrogant boasters. You will never again be arrogant on my holy mountain. I will leave within you the meek and humble and the remnant of Israel will trust in the name of Yahweh. They will do no wrong; they will not lie anymore. A dishonest tongue will not be found in their mouths. They will eat and lie down and no one will make them afraid. I will remove from you all who mourn over the loss of your appointed festivals, which is a burden and reproach for you. At that time I will deal with all who oppressed you. I will rescue the lame; I will gather the exiles. I will give them praise and honor in every land where they have suffered shame. At that time I will gather you; at that time I will bring you home. I will give you honor and praise among all the peoples of the earth when I restore your fortunes before your very eyes," says Yahweh. (Zeph 3:11–20)

It is difficult to believe that punishment and suffering can purify people. Yet we see it so often in our daily lives. The judgmental parent who critiques how others raise their children is humbled when her child is arrested, addicted, or fired from a good job. Judgmental folks are humbled when a spouse confesses to having an affair for many years. The beauty queen scarred in a car accident or the athlete who suffers a career ending injury may be humbled through suffering. Sometimes pain and oppression have a humiliating effect on people. Many times those who have lived life in arrogance and pride fall hard when justice knocks on their door.

The city of Jerusalem was arrogant, corrupt, and unjust. As Zephaniah warns the kingdom of Judah, God is just, righteous, compassionate, and faithful. God expects the world to reflect that glory, especially the people of the covenant. While surrounding armies wait to take Judah, Yahweh keeps the hostile forces at bay. However, Jerusalem does not appreciate this grace and protection and wants to "go into the world and play with these dangerous neighbors." God seeks to protect the children but instead lets them have their way. Through this process Jerusalem comes to realize that these neighboring friends don't play nice and that Yahweh was their true God.

Zephaniah, however, was not a prophet who challenged from a distance. His language suggests that he went throughout his city and called people to safety. He pleaded for the people to gather together, hide from the impending doom, and seek shelter in Yahweh. He spoke as one who was part of the suffering rather than one who from far away watched people "get what they deserved." Unlike many preachers today, Zephaniah felt that Jerusalem was his city, his people, and his problem. While God had called this prophet to warn the people and offer repentance, Zephaniah took his role personally. He suffered with them and knew that their pain was his pain. The prophet tried to rescue his people because he emotionally invested in them and considered them his people.

When I sit at Pioneer Square, I am reminded of my high school days in the small rural town of Marshall, Missouri. Every day at lunch an older woman would stand in the town square and preach. There were stores on the square as well as the post office. Many people would be out walking and driving around this square. The woman preacher would speak for twenty to forty minutes each day. Occasionally a teenager would honk. One day I sat in my truck to listen to her. She was giving what people term a fire-and-brimstone sermon. No one was listening, no one stopped, and it seemed that she was speaking into the air. As I listened, I found myself getting bored. I couldn't figure out if she was actually trying to reach people or just saying what she had to say, so she could tell others that she preached at people.

It is easy to preach *at* others. It takes courage but little relational investment. It *is their problem*, not mine. In the end, if no one cares, I've done my job and can go home with that satisfaction that others have made their own choice.

It's a different issue to preach *to* others. The call to repentance and warning of doom comes from the heart and a desire for true change. It is *our problem*. Since I am invested, it matters to me if they live or die. I don't control them or force my beliefs down their throats, but I try to persuade them because they matter to me. In the end, some care and we try to find peace and safety together because the remnant always survives. It is their choice but I am there to encourage them and help them on the journey.

PART THREE

Visionaries for Hope

8

Joel

Offering Hope during the Storm

CHARLIE WAS IN MY office with his head hung low. He was looking at the floor and kept rubbing his hands together. Andrew sat next to him, patting him on the back. I had seen Charlie's girlfriend, Cindy, two days earlier. She had come in with Sarah, Andrew's wife and Cindy's sister, because Sarah believed Cindy was addicted to meth and in an abusive relationship. Cindy was high when we met, but we tried to encourage her to leave Charlie.

"Charlie didn't mean to be abusive, it's just the drugs and booze that cause him to be that way," she kept saying. I could sense Sarah's frustration with her sister but encouraged her and Andrew to provide a safe place to talk and to give Cindy space to think clearly.

Andrew was a big guy. Charlie was lucky Andrew didn't beat him senseless over what he had done to his sister-in-law. However, Andrew and Sarah had worked with Lori and me to get Charlie and Cindy help. Andrew confronted Charlie and told him to get counseling, stop beating Cindy, and come in to see me. Charlie agreed. We were in the office, and Charlie was sharing his problems. He was heavily addicted to meth; was very angry and violent; and had a history of criminal activity, drug use, alcohol abuse, and of having been abused as a child. Charlie wanted to change.

PART THREE   Visionaries for Hope

"Charlie," I said, "I am telling you that if you do not make changes now—today, right now—you will be in prison in less than a month." Charlie nodded. Andrew put his hand on his back to support him. I told Charlie again, "We want to help you. God wants to help you. But you have to decide that you are going to do the difficult work to change the way you are living your life, the way you treat Cindy, and the children you are neglecting from your past relationships. Satan wants to take you down with him and destroy your life. God wants to bless it. But it's your choice. It's about being a man and taking responsibility for your own life."

Sometimes we have to be honest with people. Andrew was not there to sugarcoat anything. Charlie was making bad choices, and they were affecting many other people. I had seen enough men in prison to know that Charlie's life was unfolding in the same manner as other men's had who were now incarcerated. To borrow language from the prophet Joel, the sky was becoming darker, the locusts were on the horizon, and the *shophar* (horn) was blowing. We had to warn him.

We also told Charlie that things could change, that his life was not set in stone, and that he could become an important part of God's plan to help others. Charlie asked for prayer, and both Andrew and I prayed with him. I didn't feel that we had made any great changes to his life, but he left with an appointment to see me next week. As he walked outside, Cindy jumped into his arms and hugged and kissed him. She was obviously glad to see him again.

A Storm Is Brewing from the Coast

The book of Joel is another prophetic book that does not give a time frame or historical introduction. The introduction states that Joel was the son of Pethuel, but little else is known about the prophet. Since the prophet describes a great assault on Jerusalem, we can assume that the prophecy was written or given before the Babylonians attacked Jerusalem in 590 BCE—possibly during Jehoiakim's rule.[1]

Joel's description of the attack on Jerusalem was in language that was very familiar to ancient people.[2] First, the prophet pictures the armies that will attack Jerusalem as a locust invasion. Locusts are a threat in many

---

1. Crenshaw, *Prophets, Sages, and Poets*, 4.
2. For more on ancient Near Eastern texts using locusts to refer to armies see Barton, *Joel and Obadiah*, 42–46.

Joel

countries since they swarm upon the land and devour plants. They can very quickly leave a farm barren.

I grew up in the Midwest and Southern United States. I remember the cicadas (which we called locusts) when they would come out of the ground and fly in the trees. In 1998, while we lived in Missouri, the seventeen-year and thirteen-year locusts/cicadas came out together. It was a mess. Twice as many locusts as normal were out, and the trees were full of these chainsaw-sounding bugs. They would swarm people and buzz loudly, and the weight of the swarms in the trees was so heavy they would weigh down branches. Those who fished on the river were frustrated because the locusts falling from the trees were a tasty treat for the fish. My oldest son at the time was five years old, and we would pick the locusts early in the morning, as they came out of the ground and molted, and use them for bait when we went fishing that day. At nighttime we would walk in the yard and could hear the sounds of the bugs coming out of the ground. It sounded like water bubbling up from the earth. While these cicadas were harmless to humans, the swarm and noise were irritating enough to make one stay in the house. Swarming bugs can do a lot of damage, especially those that eat a community's crops.

In the book of Joel the locust army wreaked havoc upon the land by devouring living plants (1:4, 11), rushing the walls (2:9), marching to overtake a city (2:8), and covering the sun and moon, creating darkness (2:10): "They charge like warriors; they scale walls like soldiers. They stay on their course, not leaving their path" (2:7).

The locust army was also described as a nation invading Jerusalem (2:6). This nation had a powerful army that was one of the greatest in history (2:2). The description of the army as "a lion" may be an indication that this was Babylon, since the lion was the symbol for Babylon. "With a noise similar to that of chariots they leap over the mountaintops, like a blazing fire burning straw and a mighty army drawn up for battle" (2:5). This Babylonian army was led by Yahweh. God had appointed it to judge Jerusalem, and Joel saw the judgment rapidly approaching.

> Blow the horn [shophar] in Zion; sound the alarm on my holy mountain. Let all who live in the land tremble, for the day of Yahweh is coming, it's near—a day of darkness, gloom, and dark clouds. Like dawn spreading across the mountains a large and enormous army is coming, unlike what has ever been in the past or will be in the future. (2:1–2)

PART THREE   Visionaries for Hope

> Before them the earth shakes, the heavens tremble, the sun and moon are darkened, and the stars no longer shine. Yahweh roars at the head of this army; whose forces are beyond number, and who obeys God's command. The day of Yahweh is great; it is terrible. Who can endure it? (2:10–11)

Yahweh had appointed Nebuchadnezzar to lead the Babylonians into Jerusalem to punish them for their wickedness. The Day of Yahweh language reminds the people that they are being punished for their sins. This invasion would be a complete overtaking of the city. "They rush upon the city; they run along the wall. They climb into the houses; like thieves they enter through the windows" (2:9). Joel had been sent by God to share the "war weather forecast" with his people in Jerusalem. However, this weather forecast was not set in stone. The disaster could be averted. The tornado or storm clouds could dissipate. There could be hope of sunshine in dark times.

What Was the Solution?

God had sent Joel to provide an option to the doomed city. Babylon was getting ready but had not yet come. Joel called the people to mourn, and physically and publicly display repentance for their sins. The leaders could call a holiday and command everyone to cover themselves with trash bags or grocery bags and to confess their sins in the street. Everyone was suffering: livestock, fields, and families; and were called to participate in the repentance.

> Priests, put on sackcloth, mourn, and weep, you who minister before the altar. Sleep in sackcloth, you who minister before my God; for the grain offerings and drink offerings are withheld from the house of your God. Call an assembly and holy fast. Gather the elders and all who live in the land to the house of Yahweh your God, and cry out to Yahweh. (1:13–14)

There was an even greater hope that God would change the future:

> Return to me with all your heart with fasting, weeping, and mourning. Tear/rip your hearts and not your clothes. Return to Yahweh your God, who is gracious and compassionate, slow to anger and abounding in love, and changes from sending calamity. Who knows? God may change course and decide and leave behind a blessing. (2:12–14)

Joel

The people could appeal to Yahweh's nature, compassion, and code of conduct. Yahweh truly was gracious, compassionate, slow to anger, abounding in love, and could change the plan even at the last minute. Maybe they could persuade God to change the divine forecast?

Why not? It had worked for Nineveh when God sent Jonah to warn them. Jerusalem had the same opportunity. In Joel 2:1 the tornado sirens are to be sounded, and all were to gather to either see God's wrath or pray to and plead with God.

Unfortunately we know the outcome of the story.

From the other prophetic books we've read, we know that Jerusalem didn't repent. Therefore the Babylonians swarmed the city and destroyed the people. They were killed, deported, and captured. The temple was desecrated and destroyed. The altar of God was defiled, and God's special vessels were removed from the temple premises.

In spite of this, Yahweh had a plan. Did God know that the people of Judah would not repent? Probably. Did God actually believe that they could repent? Yes. While God knows the future, the prophets suggest that God leaves the future open to change. While God knows everything about us, there seem to be more times when God either chooses not to know the outcome or leaves things to chance. God has also created us as freely willing beings, each with a capacity to choose good and to bring joy to our Creator. We are not humans fulfilling a single preplanned destiny set by God. We are complex creatures reflecting the glory of our Creator and walking in the image of one who is extremely complex. While God sees the future, God leaves it open to change. While God sees our hearts, God hopes for the best in us.

We have the capacity to do good. Even when things are at their worst, we have the option to choose the good and watch the forecast change. However, when humans choose the worst, or choose not to act, God has another option. Because God knows all things, sees the future and leaves destiny open, God is aware of multiple options. Every choice we make potentially opens the door for other options. These options together create a multitude of choices, options, and new choices.

Seeing Multiple Options

My middle son and I will go to Starbucks for coffee and hot chocolate and to play with his chess set. I like taking all the boys individually for

PART THREE   Visionaries for Hope

coffee to visit with dad. Once he reached high school, my older son and I could have man-to-man discussions. The youngest one drinks hot chocolate, and we goof around. The middle one likes chess. He is smart. I have enjoyed teaching him to play chess, teaching him the names and moves of the various pieces, watching him catch on quickly, and throwing in an occasional discussion about hygiene. I told him about Bobby Fisher and how Fisher practiced with five grandmasters to prepare for the 1972 world chess championships in Iceland. The grandmasters accompanied him to the tournament and prepared him each night for his final match, against Boris Spassky.

I have also begun to show my middle son that chess is not about moves. It is about options. One does not focus on the move but on all the potential moves, their consequences, and the potential moves that each provides. Good chess players know the options. Great chess players learn to read their opponents and study all the options they themselves will have following all the potential moves their opponent might make. Chess is a game of endless possibilities, choices, options, and skill. A great chess player knows thousands of moves along with their alternative moves.

Imagine a God who knows all the possibilities that we can choose as well as all the options that will be presented to us based on each move we make. God is the ultimate chess player. God sees choices and the infinite number of alternatives that flow from these choices. God also reads human behavior. We have hope because God is not against us and we are not fulfilling one path. God is for us and continually provides choices so that we can choose to return and serve our Lord.

The people of Judah made their typical move. There were no surprises. Therefore God had another option. The people would return home after their captivity. If the impending forecast and invasion would not open their eyes, seventy years in captivity might. Then God would act. If they would not gather under the tornado sirens, then God will gather them after their exile. The invading army would be driven back (Joel 2:20), the land would become fruitful (Joel 2:21–22), the rains would return, and the crops would produce enough to pay for what had been lost (Joel 2:23–25). In the end, the people of Judah will understand and praise their God: "Then you will know that I am in Israel, that I am Yahweh your God, and that there is no other; never again will my people be shamed" (2:27).

God was dreaming of the day that they would return. The relationship would be re-established, and peace and harmony (*shalom*) would again exist. Even more than that, Yahweh would re-establish the covenant with the people:

> After this, I will pour out my Spirit on all people. Your sons and daughters will prophesy, your old men will dream dreams, your young men will see visions. Even on my servants, both men and women, I will pour out my Spirit in those days. I will display power in the sky and on the earth, blood, fire, and clouds of smoke. The sun will become dark and the moon dark red before the coming of the great and dreadful day of Yahweh. Everyone who calls on the name of Yahweh will be saved; for on Mount Zion and in Jerusalem there will be deliverance, as Yahweh has said, even among the survivors whom Yahweh calls . . . In those days and at that time, when I return the fortunes of Judah and Jerusalem, I will gather all nations and bring them down to the Valley of Jehoshaphat. (Joel 3:1—4:2)

Before we discuss the passage above, notice the symbolism or metaphors within the text. Often people see this passage as a prediction of the Christian church. The Apostle Peter did mention this text in his first sermon (Acts 2:17–28), and many believe that Peter taught that the church was the fulfillment of these passages. If by *church* we mean God's people, and by *fulfillment* we mean living out the text, then this is true. If we mean that the text pointed only to the event on Pentecost with the establishment of the Christian church, then this is not an accurate application of the Joel texts.

First, *the passages applied to a real event that the Judeans would experience when they returned from captivity*. Yahweh promises to restore Judah and Jerusalem by punishing the other kingdoms which attacked the nation. This promise occurs in other prophetic books (Obadiah, Zephaniah, and Habakkuk). When God helps the Judeans rebuild Jerusalem and their temple, God is able to judge other peoples. They too are punished for mistreating the Judeans and trafficking humans (Joel 3:3).

Second, *the language in Joel 2:28–29 is metaphorical*. As our discussion of Jeremiah showed us, the pouring out of wrath or fire or anger symbolizes judgment and punishment. Language about the pouring out or putting the Spirit symbolizes restoration of the people to God. (The Spirit is also compared to water in Isa 24; 42:1; Ezek 39:29; Mic 3:8; Zech 12:10.) The promise to bless the people and the land is followed in Joel by the promise to restore the Judeans to a relationship with Yahweh. This language is the language of healing and hope. The Spirit of God provides

PART THREE   Visionaries for Hope

this healing, reconciliation, and restoration. As Hans Walter Wolff has stated: "The pouring out of God's Spirit upon flesh means the establishment of new, vigorous life through God's unreserved giving of himself to those who, in themselves, are rootless and feeble, especially in the approaching times of judgment."[3]

Finally, *this language of healing and hope encourages the people to change their ways*. According to Joel's prophecy, instead of rebelling, the young people would preach and encourage others. Instead of nightmares the elderly will have pleasant dreams. Instead of despair the young men will have vision (Joel 2:28). God would restore all people, not just the religious leaders, and have a spirit within them. Instead of crying out to Yahweh and being ignored (Jer 11:14), the people will hear God's answer. Yahweh's intervention *this time* will bring healing, and rebuild lives and the nation. The book ended with Yahweh's judgment on other nations. This Day of Yahweh will be a day of vengeance against enemies of and protection for the Jews returning from captivity. God will prepare an army to fight, not Jerusalem, but those threatening its security. Their God will protect and save Jerusalem.

After the smoke clears, Yahweh will be seen as the all-powerful God who protects the faithful. The Judeans will know that their God lives in Jerusalem, deserves to be honored, and protects those in covenant: "Then you will know that I, Yahweh your God, dwell in Zion, my holy mountain. Jerusalem will be holy; never again will foreigners invade her. In that day the mountains will drip new wine, and the hills will flow with milk; all the ravines of Judah will run with water" (3:17–18).

According to Joel, there will be no threats, no punishment, and no outsiders oppressing the people (Joel 3:1–3). The scene is not heaven but a reminder that being faithful in relationship with Yahweh provides blessings, security, hope, and peace. God extends hope to the people of Judah, who, if they were willing to repent and return to Yahweh, would be cared for and protected (Joel 3:18-21). Regathering the people is a risk that does not guarantee renewed covenant loyalty, but God pleads that the people trust their Lord. Others gods did not have the ability to provide a future, but Yahweh did.

Often we have people come to Agape Church of Christ who struggle against addiction, who find themselves in difficult relationships, and who seek all kinds of healing in their lives. We encourage all to be part of a

---

3. Wolff, *Joel and Amos*, 60.

Joel

home community (small group), whether it is a faith-developing group, recovery group, or connecting group. Many times when people who are dealing with sin face community, they bolt. This is a term we use to describe running from a group or the church. Relationships are scary, and many who struggle to love themselves avoid being in a group of people who choose to build them up. It is difficult to understand unless you have been there. We tell people, relapse into addictive behaviors happens; and even if you sin, it's better to be part of a group there than not. We let people know that struggle with problem behavior is normal but that bolting from the group is not a good response to the struggle. However, God calls people to relationship. It was better for the Judeans to repent and seek God, even though doom lay on the horizon.

I was sitting on the couch watching the news three days after my meeting with Charlie, discussed at the start of this chapter.. The beginning of the news presents the most striking news story in our community or country. There, at the beginning of the hour, was a breaking news story. I saw Charlie's and Cindy's photos on the television. Charlie and Cindy had been arrested for murdering a prominent lawyer in Portland. The lawyer was lured by the couple for drugs in exchange for sex. Cindy had contacted him over the Internet and had arranged a meeting. When the lawyer arrived in a secluded area of Portland, both Charlie and Cindy murdered him. It was a horrible story. The events involved two people who had been in my office the past week; a lawyer, who had his own battles with addiction; and his wife and children, who had lost their father and husband as well as their sense of honor in the community. I remembered my comments to Charlie, the storm of judgment on the horizon, and the realization that Charlie's and Cindy's lives would continue. They faced life in prison as a young couple.

Since I had more of a relationship with Cindy than with Charlie (her family attended our church), I made the decision to visit her in prison. What do you say to someone who knows that you "told them so"? The only thing I could do was begin with Joel 3 and talk about hope. She could survive in prison, she could walk away from this with new resolve, she could learn lessons and rebuild her life: she could still have hope.

It was odd for me to go from predicting the storm and warning those in the image of God to painting a vision of hope and a new future. It was hard to offer hope to someone who had taken the life of a man, even if he had corrupted the law, and to leave children and a loving wife without support and with more questions than answers. It was hard to

PART THREE   Visionaries for Hope

switch from pointing the finger and narrowing my eyebrows to praying for compassion, mercy, and hope.

However, it doesn't matter if it is hard or easy.

It's what prophets are called to do.

It's who God's servants are expected to be.

9

Ezekiel

Sharing Anger, Sharing Exile, Sharing Hope

Lori and I Were Silent

WE WERE SITTING AT a funeral service for Roger, a person who had come to Agape. It was a sad time. It was our first funeral we had conducted for an adult at Agape Church.

A few months before this funeral, Roger's stepson had come to me. I had known the family for years because I had counseled them at my previous church. Lori and I had helped them with many issues over the years. We loved them and had become friends. Roger, Nancy, and her children came to Agape after our first year as a new church. Roger and Nancy had become active at Agape and had been part of our small group for many years.

Roger's stepson had come to my office because he was concerned about his sister. He felt that something had happened between his sister and Roger that had been hidden, and he wanted her to talk about it. In the past there were allegations of abuse against Roger and a legal intervention for his sister, the abuse victim; but Roger's stepson had been very young when this intervention happened, and couldn't remember much about it.

PART THREE   Visionaries for Hope

He felt that there was more that his sister needed to share. We spent time in prayer and developed a plan for him to help her with this issue.

As the months passed, their mother, Nancy, entered the discussion. Nancy had come to talk with us about how to support her daughter. She was as concerned as her son. *When Lori and I spoke, they listened.* We appreciated their willingness to work together to support the victim and confront the abuser.

An intervention occurred that included Roger, Nancy, and her son—plus one friend or family member to accompany each of them, and me. The intervention was confrontational, and many things were said in the attempt to find justice, answers, and resolution. As a trained advocate for abuse victims, I was convinced by much in the session, not only that a great sin had happened, but that its significance had been minimized. Roger lost his wife, his stepchildren, and my respect that day. Agape Church of Christ supported Nancy and her family as they stood for justice, healing, and safety. We supported Roger in his repentance and healing.

- We spoke because we could not be silent.
- Those who were victims listened.
- Roger did not.

Roger took his life a few weeks after our intervention session. He did not admit wrongdoing, nor did he apologize to his family. He just left. As a church we grieved Roger's death as well as the pain he had brought to his family. We grieved that he had hidden secrets from us and had refused help. We grieved because we also wondered if we were too hard or too unforgiving. Yet even more, we grieved over the pain of his family, all of whom were victims because of Roger's choices. We grieved because they were hurt and now would not receive validation from the one who had hurt them.

Lori and I sat at Roger's funeral, silent. Roger had left Agape Church of Christ and had begun to attend another church, where I had ministered before. During his funeral tears were shed by the speakers from that church. Those were not tears over the pain of Roger's family, over the injustice of not reaching the full truth and of not finding reconciliation with Roger, or for the other victims Roger had hurt. Those were tears over the death of this man. One eulogist compared Roger to Jesus (both were carpenters). Roger was, in this speaker's words, in heaven looking down on us. Roger was asked to say a good word to Jesus for us. There was no mention in these eulogies from members of what had been his church up to the present moment of how Roger's present and past families suffered. There was no mention that those listening to the eulogy grieved as well. Even worse, we from Agape Church of Christ were surprised that in light of all that had happened as a result of Roger's decisions, Roger was presented as a reflection of Jesus.

- We wanted to scream, but we were silent.
- We wanted to stand up and tell the people the truth; but we felt, out of respect for the family, we should hold our tongue.
- We wanted to go up front and tell his victims this is not how Jesus truly is, but we kept silent.

I wonder if we were good prophets for Jesus.

During the next few weeks after the funeral, abuse victims shared similar stories with me—stories of being silenced at the funeral of an abuser. In each of these stories, the ending was the same:

> "When they said he/she is in heaven with Jesus, I decided that I don't ever want to go there."

> "I left the church because the pastor preached my abusive mom into heaven—I said, 'I'm outta here . . .'"

> "How could my church deny my accusations against my dad? Then when he hurt someone years later, they never came to me and apologized."

Thank God that these abuse victims were talking to me about this. They were interested again in God. They were once again willing to believe. They were willing to try God a second time. They were listening.

So we continued to speak up. We spoke out. We spoke to them of the true God, the real Jesus, and the kingdom of justice.

Watching from the Camp of the Exiles

The prophet Ezekiel was a son of a priest, and probably a priest himself, who had been taken captive by the Babylonians during the first deportation from Judah. He was living near the Chebar River in Babylon when he had his first vision. (He and Daniel, as co-captives in Babylon, both had visions of Yahweh near rivers in this ancient city.) While God had left the temple at Jerusalem, Yahweh dwelled among these captives in a foreign land. Rivers were typically calm places where people gathered for prayer. Ezekiel saw a vision of God while at this river and described the moment as a time when "the hand of Yahweh was upon him." This event also occurred in other places in Ezekiel suggesting that this prophet had a strong connection to God (3:14; 8:1).

The vision of Yahweh came at a time when Ezekiel and his people felt abandoned by God. Seeing their temple destroyed, and watching the Babylonian army desecrate God's silverware as they captured the city and took the loot to their own storage chambers, and finally being transported hundreds of miles from home would have been a traumatic series of events. These acts symbolized for the Judeans that God as well as the people were powerless in mighty Babylon. So Ezekiel's vision would have been a welcome sight to this prophet who shared the fate of his people.

Yahweh appeared in a strange vision that symbolized a divine throne upon a chariot. God was both king and warrior who rode to the captives to meet them. The symbol of the rainbow (Ezek 1:28) indicated that God was still a God of the covenant, mercy, and faithfulness. Ezekiel fell down after recognizing the glory of Yahweh.

Ezekiel also heard Yahweh give him a commission to teach and preach to the captives while in Babylon. Ezekiel's vision of God included Ezekiel's own calling to be a leader among the fallen people. "Son of man, I am sending you to the Israelites, to a rebellious nation that has rebelled against me; they and their ancestors have defied me to this day. The people to whom I am sending you are stubborn faced and hard hearted. Say to them, "This is what Lord Yahweh says." Whether they listen or fail to listen—for they are rebellious—they will know that a prophet has been among them" (Ezek 2:3–6). Ezekiel's task was not dependent upon his success in winning people to his message. However, the people would know that Ezekiel was called by God simply by the message he would bring to them. His role was to let people know that a spokesman for God had been among them.

The Hebrew prophets, no matter what their setting—Jerusalem or Babylon—spoke to an inattentive audience. In the first vision, Ezekiel was also reminded that his role was dependent upon his obedience to Yahweh. Yahweh told Ezekiel that he was a watchman and would be accountable for warning people of the impending fall of Jerusalem (Ezekiel 3; 34). If he warned someone, and they ignored his voice, they were responsible for their own life. But if the prophet failed to warn, and the hearers died, the prophet was accountable for their death:

> Son of man, I have made you a watchman for Israel; so listen to me and warn them. When I say to a wicked person, "You will die," and you do not warn them or speak out to call them to change their evil ways in order to save their life, that wicked person will die for their sin, and I will hold you accountable for their blood. But if you warn the wicked person and they do not turn from their evil ways, they will die for their sin; but you will have saved yourself. When a righteous person turns and does evil, and I put a stumbling block before them, they will die. Since you did not warn them, they will die for their sin. The righteous things that person did will not be remembered, and I will hold you accountable for their blood. But if you warn the righteous person and they do not sin, they will live because they took warning, and you will have saved yourself. (Ezek 3:16–21)

Ezekiel had to fulfill his calling by speaking the truth to a people in great danger. But Yahweh would not abandon him as Jerusalem had been abandoned. Yahweh's Spirit attended to the prophet as he sat among his people and felt the pain of God's heart. "The hand of Yahweh was on me there, and said to me, 'Get up and go out to the plain, and there I will speak to you.' So I got up and went out to the plain and the glory of Yahweh was standing there, like the glory I had seen by the Kebar River, and I fell facedown. Then the Spirit came into me and raised me to my feet" (Ezek 3:22–24).

Ezekiel carried the weight of his people and the heart of God. He lived in exile, but Yahweh proved to be in exile with the people as well. The prophet was to share the dreaded news that Jerusalem, even though it survived the devastation from Babylon, would not recover and would eventually be seized again. Ezekiel used three sermon illustrations to drive the point home to the people. First, he built a model of Jerusalem under siege, laying on each side near the model for a prescribed number of days to symbolize the two deportations of Jews to Babylon. Second, he ate small rations and cooked his food over dung with fear and trembling, to symbolize the fear of captivity. In a final sermon illustration, Ezekiel shaved his head and divided the hair into three parts. One part he burned, another part he scattered, and a third part he further divided with a sword. From among this final part, Ezekiel tucked a small amount in his garment; this fraction represented the remnant of people who would be saved in order to rebuild the city one day. Enacting three prophetic gestures or 'sermon illustrations' communicated in the ancient Near East a prophecy's authority and legitimacy.[1]

Yahweh Cares Enough to Give Warning

Yahweh spoke to the people to declare that they were being divinely punished for their rebellion and injustices.

> You have been worse than the nations around you and have not followed my decrees or kept my laws. You have not even conformed to the standards of the nations around you. This is what Lord Yahweh says: "I personally am against you, Jerusalem, and I will inflict punishment on you in the sight of the nations/gentiles. Because of all your detestable idols, I will do to you what I have never done before and will never do again. In your presence parents will eat their children, and children will eat their parents. I will punish you and will scatter all your survivors to the winds. Because you have defiled my sanctuary with all your evil images and disgusting practices, I personally will shave you; I will not look on you with pity or spare you. A third of your people will die of the plague or perish by famine inside you; a third will fall by the sword outside your walls; and a third I will scatter to the winds. Then my anger will cease and my wrath against them will subside, and I will be vindicated." (Ezek 5:7–13)

The land would suffer this punishment because Israel violated the covenant. Even though God's issue was with the people, the inhabited land would suffer destruction. For Ezekiel it was important to communicate that this punishment would come at the hands of Yahweh. While Nebuchadnezzar, the Babylonian army, and mercenaries from other nations would be the culprits, Yahweh was directly in charge of this assault and divine punishment. Yahweh was "unleashing anger" (Ezek 7:3), "handing [the people] over" (7:21), and "dealing [with the people] according to their own sins" (7:27). Why was Yahweh so willing to act this way? Because the people needed to know who Yahweh was (7:27). Yahweh was honorable and would fulfill the covenant terms as promised. God was taking responsibility for the punishment Judah had faced.

---

1. We know this especially from ancient texts uncovered at Mari. See Nissinen, *Prophets and Prophecy in the Ancient Near East*, 22–28.

To some readers today, Yahweh's behavior seems violent and controlling. We must remember the bigger picture. Israel had habitually violated the relationship of love, trust, intimacy, and faithfulness with its God (Ezek 16:15–36). Israel was abusive, dismissive, controlling, and oppressive of God and of the least in its society. Yahweh was now, after centuries of this abuse, finally acting with justice. Instead of holding back the forces of evil that so desperately wanted to exterminate the people, Yahweh stopped intervening. God gave Israel what they wanted: an abusive and violent lover. While God is often blamed for the punishment in the prophets, it was Israel and Babylon who were the guilty and violent parties.

Yahweh Shows Prophets the Truth

Yahweh again appeared to Ezekiel while he was sitting with the elders of the community. He was transported, in the vision, to Jerusalem to see the sins of the city. How sad it must have been for Ezekiel to realize that those remaining in Jerusalem had not learned their lesson from the previous deportation! The prophet witnessed the "idol of jealousy" (Hebrew: "image of anger"), which was so repulsive that Yahweh left the temple (Ezek 8:4). The Jerusalem elders were worshiping false gods in enclosed rooms in the temple (8:9–10). Women were weeping for the pagan god Tammuz (8:12–13), and twenty-five men were worshiping the sun at the entrance to the sanctuary (8:16). In addition, violence continued throughout the city (8:17). It was clear: the people had rejected God (8:6).

Yahweh decided to act. A messenger was sent into the city to put a mark or a seal on those still faithful to Yahweh and then to cut the rest of the people down with the sword: "I will not look on them with pity or spare them, I will bring down on their own heads what they have done" (Ezek 9:10). Ezekiel told his audience in exile that God would take the city of Jerusalem captive. The prophet dug through the wall of his home and assembled his belongings to illustrate that those still in Jerusalem would be transported to Babylon. Even if the king escaped the city, Yahweh planned to have him captured: "They will know that I am Yahweh, when I scatter them among the nations and throughout the countries. I will spare a few of them from the sword, famine, and plague, so that in the nations where they go they may acknowledge all their detestable practices. Then they will know that I am Yahweh" (12:15–16). It was necessary

PART THREE   Visionaries for Hope

for them to understand Yahweh's honor, however, God promised to spare some of the faithful in order to rebuild the city.

Other prophets were telling the people that God would save them. These were proclaiming that Yahweh would defeat Babylon and that there would be peace. Yet God called them false prophets and sent Ezekiel to confront them and to warn the people not to listen to them. In the end, the fall of Jerusalem proved these other voices false (Ezek 13:10). While it seems cruel that God would allow people to be deceived, Ezekiel reminds us that people will listen to what they want to believe. Three times Yahweh mentioned that they had set up idols in their hearts (Ezek 14:3,4,7). However, in the end, the righteous would be saved by their faith and trust (14:20). God promised to save a remnant from the burning/fire upon the city (15:7).

God compared Jerusalem to an abandoned child found on the road, saved, raised in love, and married off in faithfulness (Ezekiel 16). Given that Yahweh always provided for the weak, the small remnant of Israel was also cared for by the Creator. Unfortunately the kingdom (child) became unfaithful and ungrateful to Yahweh and had sexual affairs with other gods/kingdoms. In Ezek 16:25, Yahweh's wife (Israel) was not only promiscuous, but she was a sex addict, seeking fulfillment everywhere but with the one who offered true love. This unfaithfulness involved not only idolatry but social injustice. "Samaria did not commit half the sins you did. You have done more detestable things than they, and have made your sisters seem righteous by all these things you have done. Bear your disgrace, for you have furnished some justification for your sisters. Because your sins were viler than theirs, they appear more righteous than you. So then, be ashamed and bear your disgraces, for you have made your sisters appear righteous" (Ezek 16:49–52).

The spouse of God had broken the marriage covenant (16:15) and deserved punishment. They were oppressive not only to their God but also to those who were dependant on community justice. However the people continued to blame others for their sin: "What do you people mean by quoting this proverb about the land of Israel: 'The parents eat sour grapes, and the children's teeth are set on edge'?" (Ezek 18:2).

Yahweh was fair and just. Those who sinned suffered for their own actions. God wanted the nation to choose right and be blessed. Yahweh exhibited love not because the people were disciplined. Rather God exhibited love by means of giving the people the opportunity to choose to change their behavior and do what was right.

> "Do I take pleasure in the death of the wicked?" declares Lord Yahweh. "I am pleased when they turn from their ways and live." (Ezek 18:23)

> You say, "The way of Yahweh is not fair." Am I unfair? Isn't it you who are unfair? Therefore, you Israelites, I will judge each of you according to your own ways, declares Lord Yahweh. Repent! Turn away from all your offenses; then sin will not be your downfall. Rid yourselves of all the offenses you have committed, and get a new heart and a new spirit. Why will you die, people of Israel? For I take no pleasure in the death of anyone . . . Repent and live! (Ezek 18:25–32)

The exiles in Babylon prepared to mourn the dark history of Jerusalem. There would be no hope for the city, only suffering. Like a Marilyn Manson song, this lament was filled with violence, fear, anger, and rage.

The elders in exile came to question Ezekiel. One wonders if they were moved by the prophet's scathing critique concerning their honesty and faithfulness to Yahweh. However, the prophet confirmed to them that God would punish the city of Jerusalem for its sin. While the exiles in Babylon may have heard Nebuchadnezzar and the Babylonian people discuss Jerusalem's future, Yahweh was clear: Nebuchadnezzar would not make the call to go to battle; it would be Yahweh's decision to lead the army to victory (Ezek 21:19–23). The Judeans still had not learned their lesson and needed to be humbled, again (22:23–31).

Even though God had left survivors in Jerusalem, they still had chosen to rebel and turn away from Yahweh. They had become flagrant in their disobedience so that Yahweh took the behavior personally. Yahweh was offended, so their God decided to personally hand out punishment: "They have also done this to me; at that same time they defiled my sanctuary and desecrated my Sabbaths. On the very day they sacrificed their children to their idols, they entered my sanctuary and desecrated it. That is what they did in my house" (Ezek 23:38–40).

God had been attacked and disgusted by their behavior. Not only was God acting as a hurt spouse, but God was suffering the continual offense and rejection of a people who turned their back on their Creator. It was not God's desire to understand why they behaved as they did; God wanted to end the pain. Ezekiel's wife was to die while in captivity. The prophet was forbidden to mourn over her death (Ezek 24:15). This refusal to grieve would be highly inappropriate but a sign to others that God would not mourn the loss of Jerusalem (24:25–27).

PART THREE   Visionaries for Hope

In the book of Ezekiel Jerusalem is called "the city of bloodshed," indicating that injustice continued to happen even after the first deportation of residents to Babylon. Ezekiel also compares the city to a pot of meat that when emptied contains a layer of residue on the edges. The pot must be heated to remove the residue (Ezek 11:7). The next attack of Nebuchadnezzar was designed to remove the remnant who remained in Jerusalem and still continued to rebel against Yahweh.

Watching the Nations

The prophet then turns his attention to the foreign communities outside Judah. This section of Ezekiel's prophecy, similar to sections of other prophetic books, features warnings from Yahweh (Ezekiel 25–32). Since Nebuchadnezzar was God's servant to punish Jerusalem for idolatry and injustice, God would use the same king to judge other peoples in the region around Judah. The Ammonites, Moabites, Edomites, and Philistines would all suffer the same fate as Jerusalem because they laughed at its punishment.

More powerful communities were also punished by God. Tyre, a powerful merchant city, was crushed due to their pride and rejection of Yahweh. While some believe that the king of Tyre represents Satan (due to the language of Ezekiel 27), the text does not tell us this. Tyre's king, like many others, had set himself up as a god and would be brought down by the true God. Pharaoh and Egypt are compared to a great river monster dragged out of the river by Yahweh. (Egypt depended on the Nile for most of its livelihood.) As God personally claimed responsibility for the fall of Jerusalem, so Yahweh went head to head with the mighty powers of the world.

After God predicted Jerusalem's punishment, Ezekiel was reminded that he had a calling. He was a watchman called to warn and encourage the exiles. The response of the exiles was upon their own heads, but Ezekiel was given a mission: to warn the nations. Being a prophet involved a serious charge. When Ezekiel was first called as a prophet, he had just witnessed the glory of Yahweh. The prophet's final reminder also preceded the glory of the New Jerusalem.

Judgment Begins With Leadership

Months after calling Ezekiel to act as a watchman, God reminded the prophet that his role was to warn the leaders (shepherds) to repent. Ezekiel 34 is Yahweh's challenge to the religious leaders:

> Son of man, prophesy against the shepherds of Israel; prophesy and say to them, "This is what Lord Yahweh says: Woe to the shepherds of Israel who only take care of themselves. The shepherds should take care of the flock. You eat the curds, use the wool for clothes and slaughter the best animals, but you do not care for the flock. You have not strengthened the weak or healed the sick or bound up the injured. You have not brought back the strays or searched for the lost. You have ruled them harshly and brutally. So they were scattered because there was no shepherd, and when they were scattered they became food for all the wild animals. My sheep wandered over all the mountains and on every high hill. They were scattered over the whole earth, and no one searched or looked for them. Hear the word of Yahweh, you shepherds. As I live," declares sovereign *Yahweh*, "because my flock does not have a shepherd and so has been plundered and become food for all wild animals, because my shepherds did not search from my flock but cared for themselves rather than for my flock, therefore, shepherds, hear the word of Yahweh ... I am against the shepherds and will hold them accountable for my flock. I will remove them from shepherding the flock so that the shepherds can no longer feed themselves. I will rescue my flock from their mouths, and it will no longer be food for them ... I will search for my sheep and care for them." (Ezek 34:1–11)

The Israelite leaders were condemned for their failure to imitate God's leadership methods: They had failed as leaders because they cared for themselves and neglected the sheep (Ezek 34:2–4). The leaders also failed to practice relational leadership by neglecting the injured and stray sheep. They did not strengthen the weak, heal the sick, bind up the injured, bring back the strays, and search for the lost. They were harsh in their treatment of God's people (34:4). Because of their selfishness and neglect the sheep were scattered and open to predators (34:5–6). God was angry because these leaders were given the responsibility to care for God's sheep. Since God guided, fed, nurtured, and protected the people, the leaders were expected to do the same. Israelite leadership failed to imitate God's care and concern for the people and as a result God's people strayed from the faith and were sent to captivity.

God then intervened into this dysfunctional system. First, *God held the shepherds accountable for their actions*, destroyed the strong, and judged the leaders (Ezek 34:10, 16, 17–22). They were removed from leadership so that the sheep could be rescued (34:10). God also sought out the stray sheep (34:11–14). God was practicing *oversight* and a willingness to painstakingly search out the needs of the flock. (This concept of oversight is central to the meaning of our word *bishop*.) The Babylonian captivity was God's opportunity to remove the corrupt leaders and gather the faithful remnant.

Second, *God promised to bind the injured and strengthen the weak* (Ezek 34:15). Yahweh's oversight and care would strengthen the weak and judge the strong. God promised to restore the sheep by searching for the lost and shepherding them with justice (34:15–17). God would provide for their needs and care for them rather than oppress them. As the people of Judah were led home to rebuild their city, Yahweh proved to be their shepherd who was to establish a covenant of peace, safety, and knowledge of Yahweh (34:25, 28, 30).

The land suffered from the destruction of Jerusalem. Israel's defiance against Yahweh affected both humans and the rest of creation. The devastation was so heavy that Ezekiel described the sight as a "valley of dry bones" (see Ezekiel 37). The prophet, however, provided hope for the people. Not only was the prophet called to warn. He was called to speak words of healing and power. The city of Jerusalem, symbolized by the slaughtered bones, would once again come to life through the Word of Yahweh and the Holy Spirit. God's spirit would resurrect the fallen nation and unite the two separated kingdoms.

> Then he said to me: "Son of man, these bones are the people of Israel. They say, 'Our bones are dried up and our hope is gone; we are cut off.' Therefore prophesy and say to them: 'This is what Lord Yahweh says: My people, I am going to open your graves and bring you up from them; I will bring you back to the land of Israel. Then you, my people, will know that I am Yahweh, when I open your graves and bring you up from them. I will put my Spirit in you and you will live, and I will settle you in your own land. Then you will know that I Yahweh have spoken, and I have done it, declares Yahweh.'" (Ezek 37:11–14)
>
> I will take the Israelites out of the nations where they have gone. I will gather them from all around and bring them back into their own land. I will make them one nation in the land, on the

Ezekiel

mountains of Israel. There will be one king over all of them and they will never again be two nations or be divided into two kingdoms. (Ezek 37:21-22)

God's Spirit was a promised gift to the exiles and remnant. This Spirit would not only heal the wounded nation but would restore their relationship to God.

I will restore the fortunes of Jacob and will have compassion on all the people of Israel, and I will be zealous for my holy name. They will forget their shame and all the unfaithfulness they showed toward me when they lived in safety in their land with no one to make them afraid. When I have brought them back from the nations and have gathered them from the countries of their enemies, I will be proved holy through them in the sight of many nations. Then they will know that I am Yahweh their God, for though I sent them into exile among the nations, I will gather them to their own land, not leaving any behind. (Ezek 39:25-28)

The Spirit also provided life and reminded the newly resettled people that Yahweh continued to live among them: "The name of the city from that time on will be: Yahweh is there" (48:35). The book ended with a detailed description of the new city and temple. While not meant to be literal, the dimensions, construction, and materials were exaggerated to suggest, as did Haggai, that this new life would be better than the first life.

Ezekiel's prophecy is a powerful reminder that prophets are called not just to warn others but to give them a vision of hope. Ezekiel's relationship with Yahweh allowed him to have insight into the hidden secrets of those in captivity and the remnant in Jerusalem.

Modern Prophets and People in Exile

Leonora Tubbs Tisdale believes that the church today, much like Ezekiel in captivity, must call God's people to return to their relationship with their Lord:

I personally believe that what the church today most longs for are visionary leaders who speak to their people of an alternative future that can be believed and embraced and lived in like much of society around us the church can easily fall prey to its cynicism and despair. But the best antidote to such despair and

PART THREE   Visionaries for Hope

cynicism is that alternate vision of God we glimpse the Gospel: a vision of a universe made new, whole, and fresh by a God who loves it inordinately and will not rest until that which is upside down is turned right side up—until the justice, righteousness, and *shalom* of God cover the earth as the waters cover the sea.[2]

Ezekiel was commissioned as a watchman to both warn the people of God and encourage them with hope. In the midst of these warnings was a cry from a God who asked people to return. Yahweh not only left the temple because the Babylonians destroyed the building, God left because Judah had driven out their Lord. The "image of anger" (possibly referring to Asherah) was a slap in Yahweh's face, a kick to God's groin, and a "giving the finger" to the Creator of the universe. Judah had spoken, therefore Ezekiel was sent to speak for Yahweh. While the captivity was a sign that God had spoken, the message of Ezekiel was that Yahweh continued to work. No matter what the people of Judah chose to do, Ezekiel was to remind them that God was still present.

The prophet's gloom is mixed with hope, vision, and a desire for change. Through Ezekiel the nation knew that God longed for relationship, that God wanted them back, and that God had a vision of new life. The new temple and filling by the spirit suggested that Yahweh's relationship was renewable and open for forgiveness.

Today many need to know that prophets have been among them. However, prophets must *be among them*. As a minister I have found it difficult to call Jesus's people out of the church buildings, Christian institutions, and safety of our Christian homes to engage others in our communities. The missional, emerging/emergent, and missional-incarnational movements in Christianity have called Christians to engage people in their communities. Attractional ministries ask, "How do we get people to come here?" Missional communities ask, "Where can we meet people?" Ezekiel reminds us that God and God's prophet lived among the exiles. Ezekiel lived among the captives and heard their questions, complaints, and fears. Yahweh called him to live among the people so that he could address their questions. There were no temple or priests to seek out, all of these had become corrupt and unclean. However, God continued to connect with those who lived on the margins by preparing and sending a prophet who would both challenge them and offer them hope.

2. Tisdale, *Prophetic Preaching*, 37.

The Spirit acts as a force that not only offered healing and hope of reconciliation. The Spirit enables communication between God and those in the camp. Through this Yahweh held out hope of relationship and love. God desired to be known and honored in the world.

Today God continues to pursue people. Not just in order to make them feel better but in order to show love and power to others who need to know Yahweh and develop relationship. God is truly among people. We as prophets are also called to be among them. While we are called to warn, we are most importantly called to give hope, provide a vision of what could be, and remind people that God pursues them. People should know that they have a responsibility to return their love to God, who blesses us daily.

We should ask: do others know that a prophet of God is among them?

10

Haggai

Replacing Shame with Hope in a New Life

I HAVE TAUGHT THE exilic and postexilic prophets to undergraduates at a Christian college. This was an upper-level class that required the students to have their Introduction to Bible classes completed. Because it was an upper-level class, I always enjoyed the class discussions, especially when we studied Haggai. We would usually begin by discussing their reading. Since this prophetic book was only two chapters long, I knew that the students would have appreciated that week's preparation. According to the class, it was obvious that God was frustrated with the state of the country. Judah had returned home from Babylon and been asked to build God's temple and the wall to the city. Unfortunately this had not happened. The people had become distracted. They had focused on their homes, paneling their walls (Hag 1:4), a luxury practiced earlier by King Jehoiakim as well (Jer 22:14). They had planted their crops, built their barns, and been preparing for a great harvest. The people, instead of focusing on God's house, had expended their energy getting their own lives in order. They had, once again, neglected their Lord.

In Ezra 4:24 the Judeans were forced by the Persian officials to stop building their temple. Even though they were sent home by the Persian king Cyrus, area opponents petitioned the Persian officials to intervene in the work. By 520 BCE, the second year of Darius the King of Persia, the

Judeans were given permission to rebuild. However, God, through Haggai, did not excuse them for neglecting to rebuild this city and temple. In Jerusalem they continued to rebuild their houses but avoided the house of Yahweh. God reminded them that all their energies were futile. While they had redecorated their homes and updated their farming techniques, they were still not being blessed. The author of their blessings was supposed to be God, not their social status in society. Throughout Haggai chapter 1, God reminded the people that they were focused on themselves rather than their Lord. Their relationship with God was suffering because they continued to chase their own comfort and success. This in turn, kept them from being who they needed to be.

> Now this is what Yahweh Almighty says: "Think about what you are doing. You have planted much, but harvested little. You eat, but never have enough. You drink, but are still in need. You put on clothes, but are not warm. You earn wages, only to put them in a purse with holes in it." (1:5–6)

> This is what Yahweh Almighty says: "Think about what you are doing. Go up into the mountains and bring down timber and build my house, so that I may take pleasure in it and be honored," says Yahweh. "You expected much, but have received little. What you brought home, I blew away. Why? Because my house is still a wreck, and each of you is busy with your own house. Because of you there is no rain and the earth does not produce crops. I called for a drought on the fields and the mountains, on the grain, the new wine, the olive oil and everything else the ground produces, on people and livestock, and on all the labor of your hands." (1:7–11)

God's repeated phrase in these two passages, "think about what you are doing" (take this to heart), indicates that the returnees to Jerusalem needed to reflect on what was or was not happening. Even though the Persian government commanded them to cease building the temple, God had not given them permission to stop. God was in charge of the Persian government and called Israel to listen to Yahweh, not the king.

After this introduction to the discussion of Haggai, I ask the students in my class why the people neglected God's temple. The students are always willing to share their answers. They suggest that the people ignored God because they were lazy, selfish, greedy, unspiritual, stupid, and so on. The class seems to enjoy attacking the people because it is always safe for us to blame others for their sin without looking at our own.

PART THREE   Visionaries for Hope

It is also the way we have typically been taught to read a biblical text. We remove ourselves from the story, therefore removing our emotional connection to what others are doing. In this case, we read our anger as equal to God's anger. According to this understanding of the story, we read God's words as judgmental and condemning. God seems to be scolding the people for being afraid of their Persian king.

"So what was God's solution?" I ask.

The class responds that God warned them, threatened them, and watched them. The passages express God's call to the city:

- I am with you (1:13) . . . I'm watching you
- Yahweh stirred up their spirit (1:14) . . . Yahweh goaded them to action
- Work, for I am with you (2:4) . . . Get to work!
- Take this to heart (1:5,7) . . . Use your head and think about this
- Do not be afraid (2:5) . . . Man up!

To my students these verses suggest that God was willing to motivate these "unfaithful people," through challenges, to do what they were supposed to do. Like a drill sergeant who pushes soldiers to their capacity using shame and humiliation, God reminded them that they were lazy and neglectful. They let others intimidate them, thereby proving that the Jewish people were cowards. We all seemed satisfied in the class to determine that the book of Haggai challenged the people to "snap out of it" and get busy working.

The Story through the Eyes of Shame

After we have this discussion in class, I ask the students to try looking at the book in a different way. I mention that the temple was still in ruins at the heart of the city. I suggest that every day the people were reminded of their sin and their fathers' sins as they passed by the rubble. I ask what it would be like to walk by the destruction and think, "We screwed up big time; it's our fault the temple was crushed"; or, "look what we did to a loving God." I ask my students what it is like to be reminded every day that your choices, or the choices of others, wrecked a relationship. Is it any different to hear:

- Every time I come to my home church, I am reminded how I hurt my parents when I walked away.
- When I have visitation of my kids, I see that their foster parent treats them better than I ever did.
- When I see my ex-spouse, I am reminded how my drug use and abuse ruined her life and the lives of her family.
- I used to be clean, I used to go to church, I used to pray to God; now I'm just used.
- I had an affair on the person God put in my life.
- I gambled away my kids' college fund.
- I was baptized, then started smoking pot; the rest is history.
- I let a bully keep me from having a wonderful life.

It is interesting to watch my students' faces as I share this with them. I see in their eyes the realization that Haggai may not involve an angry God yelling at sinful, rebellious people. God may not be the drill sergeant whipping the lazy recruits into shape. I then ask my class how easy it was for the people of Judah to focus on their houses when they wanted to avoid working on the broken temple, which they believed they had wrecked. The students respond that maybe the people in Haggai's day were too ashamed to take care of God's business so they played it safe and focused on home improvement. I ask them:

- What is it like to be paralyzed with fear?
- What does it mean to live in shame?
- How did guilt and regret color my vision of holiness.

Shame is a feeling that says, I am bad. Guilt states, I have done badly. Unfortunately guilt feeds shame for many people, instead of motivating them to change. For those steeped in shame and self-loathing, guilt only drives them deeper into sadness. For those overcome with fear, guilt makes them more afraid. Even more, it provides a convenient excuse to avoid that which is good.

- Why do women leaving abuse so often quickly hook up with another abuser?
- Why do many rape victims self-medicate?

- Why do people brought up in dysfunction repeat that pattern with their families?
- Why do people in pain self-injure?
- Why do victims of affairs feel that they need to make themselves more attractive to their spouse?

Fear. Shame. Guilt. All these drive people from that which is good. The Holy One is pure, good, loving, and powerful; but for those living in fear, the thought of relationship with pure love is too intimidating. It does not motivate. It is only a reminder that one is a failure. The verses in Haggai that suggest on the surface that God is motivating people to get to work actually reveal something more.

A Modern Story of Shame, Fear, and Avoidance

"Ron, I need to talk to you," the voice said on the other end of the phone. Shelly was baptized a year earlier by my wife, Lori. One of our former street kids who checked into a drug treatment program brought Shelly to church one Sunday. Shelly was in treatment for heroin and meth addiction, had lost her children, and had spent months in prostitution. Through time, her hard work, and the energy of a loving church, Shelly had her children returned, left treatment, and had been placed in an apartment. We all loved Shelly and worked to help her put her life back together. She was eager to learn about God and be baptized into Jesus. However, over the months it became difficult for her to stay clean, to be devoted to her children, and to look for a job. Shelly would share with us that a man was showing her a lot of attention, buying her expensive gifts, and watching the children while she went out. We knew what was happening. Even though Shelly claimed to never need a pimp (she could handle herself with any John and would rather take the risk of that than an abusive pimp), we saw it coming. One day she was gone, lost the kids, and would not return our phone calls or text messages. She was hooked by a pimp and was in danger.

Two months later Shelly had called us. She knew she could reach out to us and knew Agape would be a safe place for her to return. That typically seems to be how it happens. When we are too ashamed to face God or those we have hurt, we focus inward. Sometimes we work to preserve our dignity by criticizing others. We are harsh with other people because we hate ourselves. We stay home, repaint our spiritual houses monthly, and keep others away. The people of Haggai's day may have been overwhelmed with shame and guilt. Maybe God was like a coach, encouraging and motivating them to work on God's temple.

A coach's best gift is the ability to inspire people to work hard and enjoy a sport. I loved sports when I was younger. I had lousy coaches and good coaches. The good coaches could get me to do anything for them at practice because I respected them and knew that they wanted me to be the best. The lousy coaches didn't create a relationship with many of us on the team. I have read that a prominent university men's basketball coach would put a tampon in a player's locker if he felt the player didn't perform well enough. He found a way to shame them by degrading women and those who don't "measure up." Good coaches encouraged and supported us to do our best. They were there for us when we failed and found a way to help us learn from our mistakes. Over the years I have used what they taught me when I have coached kids' sports, refereed high school wrestling, and mentored others in ministry. Guilt does not motivate people to succeed.

God responds to the Jerusalem people by developing relationship with them. The night Shelly called was a joy to us, because we knew she was alive and still seeking God.

"Shelly, is that you?" I asked. "Everyone at Agape misses you."

"I know," she said. As her voice cracked she blurted out, "I miss my kids, I want them back, I want to come home, I don't want to 'work' any more" (a term she used for prostituting). "I want to leave my pimp." I listened as she repeated some of those phrases over again. Lori and I had prayed that she would call, come back, and give her life back to God.

We knew that the problem was not her prostitution. Shelly lives in a world where men and women approve of other women selling sex for money. Some men condition women (as well as girls and boys) to willingly open themselves sexually to another person. This conditioning requires rape, coercion, abuse, and torture: whatever it takes to make a person offer up something designed for intimacy. Some men pay money to the woman and her pimp for their own gratification. They destroy themselves and their victims. Other men actively view pornography. While popular sitcoms suggest that it is healthy for married males to have their pornographic magazines, visit strip clubs, or view pornography on the Internet, pornography is similar to prostitution. There exists

PART THREE Visionaries for Hope

a pimp (the producer) and john (the consumer) and a victim. Orgasm is achieved through exploitation rather than love and affection.

Other men turn their heads to this issue and pretend it doesn't exist. They laugh at the jokes about women. They support the belief that men are brute beasts driven by sex. Even worse, other people blame the victim. The woman, girl, or boy selling sex is exploited; each is the victim of systemic, cultural, and gender perceptions that encourage the belief that males have the right to be sexually satisfied by another individual without the cost of intimacy, romance, love, and commitment. Shelly, like many others, lives in this system and has found a way to survive. As usual, the system beat Shelly, but she wanted to return to the other system that offered unconditional love, hope, and acceptance.

"Shelly," I interrupted, "no matter what you have done, no matter what has happened, no matter how bad it looks, you know Lori and I love you."

"Yes, I know," she said.

"You know you can always come back to Agape and we will walk with you in this journey," I said.

"Yes," she sobbed.

"You know that God deeply loves you and wants you in relationship and wants you to be safe," I said.

At that point she was silent, then said, "I gotta go. I'll call you later."

It is hard to believe that God loves and cares about us. It is hard to believe that the Creator of all life and the universe, who sees all and knows all, and who rules the world can passionately seek relationship with those who, being in God's image, sin and ruin their own lives. It's even harder to embrace this love and live in relationship with an awesome Lord.

Shelly, like the people of Haggai's day, struggled with forgiveness. While she made choices and suffered the consequences of those choices, she found (like many of us) that it was easier to avoid God than to be in the divine being's presence. The difficult tasks of detoxifying, getting sober, being responsible, working to retrieve the children, and staying clean can become our focus even at the expense of reviving our relationship with God. Guilt and shame can, in addition to this, become motivating forces keeping us from our loving God.

The relationship with our God, however, can be a motivating force to help us in the difficult journey of rebuilding our lives. God's Spirit is given to those in the kingdom to draw them closer in relationship to Yahweh. In Haggai's day Yahweh worked with the people.

- "I am with you" (Hag 1:13; 2:4,5).
- God stirred up the spirit of the leaders to set the pace (Hag 1:13).
- God encouraged them to be strong (Hag 2:4).
- God reminded them that they had relationship/covenant (Hag 2:5).

God's response was to encourage them to think about their future. The Hebrew phrase "Give careful thought to your ways" (Hag 1:5, 7) meant, "take this to heart." Yahweh wanted them to take a good look at their lives and choices. In all their efforts to avoid God, they had become miserable. They, like so many people I know, tried to run from the one who cares for us the most. It is easier to hide than face Yahweh. God's house remained in ruins because they had become overwhelmed with shame and guilt.

Hope Inspires Vision; Vision Inspires Hope

God gave Haggai's crowd a vision for something better. While they saw the ruins of the temple, God saw the potential for a new temple. While they saw a people who stopped working due to the decree of the Persian ruler, God saw a nation ready to be blessed by a new ruler. While shame drove them to focus on home improvement, God's Spirit drove them to reconnect with their Lord. God used the prophet Haggai to encourage the team to rebuild and renew their courage.

First, Haggai reminded them that *God was with them* (Hag 1:13). Just as God had promised to be with Moses, Joshua, David, Hezekiah, Jehoshaphat, Josiah, and others, so God reminded the people of Haggai's day that they would not be abandoned. While the captivity was a reminder that God had cut ties with Israel, this was a new time, and God would once again initiate the relationship. God inspired the leaders of the returnees, such as the governor Zerubbabel and the priest Joshua, to lead them forward. God not only walked with them, but God inspired others to walk with them as well. The nation was once again feeling the blessings of their relationship with God.

Second, God *encouraged them to dream again concerning their future.* Fifty-one days after Yahweh addressed the people (Hag 2:1), God spoke to them and asked them to be courageous. While some may have remembered the glory of the original temple, all would have remembered the shame of the rubble. However, God reminded them that the future

PART THREE   Visionaries for Hope

was hopeful. God called them three times to "be strong" (2:4), reminded them that they were not alone and that the Spirit was with them, promised a relationship, and encouraged them to not be afraid (2:5). God not only wanted the returnees from Babylon to succeed, God wanted them to believe that they could succeed.

While the future would have been uncertain for the people who saw the temple destroyed, feared the Persian king who halted their work, and was overcome with shame, God intended for them to have a vision. The Jews had seen God work in bringing them home through the hand of the Persian king Cyrus; but they had experienced conflict in building this temple. However, God called them to look to the future. God gave them a vision of hope: "The glory of this house [temple] will be greater than the glory of the former house [temple] . . . " (Hag 2:9). God also promised to bring peace to the city of Jerusalem. For a people who had seen war, destruction, displacement, shame, and sin, the ability to hope in something greater than the original temple and city of Jerusalem would have been too difficult to imagine.

Finally, in response to this people's lack of hope for the future, *God gave them a new start*. Sixty-three days after they were given the vision of hope (Hag 2:10), God sent Haggai to their priests. In Hag 2:10–19 God used the illustration of clean and unclean as a metaphor for the nation. The priests knew that infection was passed from unclean to clean. Infection spreads when healthy tissue comes in contact with diseased tissue. Clean tissue, food, or objects do not cleanse things that are unclean, that can only be done through a powerful agent. However, unclean objects easily infect others. The priests knew that clean tissue and food can only be infected by something unholy. God reminded them that this was the case. For the Israelite priests the question remained, if we are all unclean and separated from God due to our sins, how do we (who are priests) make others clean? The people of Israel had to face this question, which may have been a reason they did not want to rebuild the temple.

God had a solution: since the unclean can only be sanitized through a solvent, "I will clean all things." God again asked the leaders twice to reflect or "give careful thought" (Hag 2:18). They were to remember that they could not become clean, that they were infected, and that there was no hope in themselves for salvation. However, God responded: "From this day on, I will bless you" (2:19). There it was. God did not plan to cleanse them, call them to more work, or even reboot their hard drive. God decided to bless them. Whether or not they were worthy was up to

Yahweh. However, their God knew that a new start would require a new blessing, a new hope, and a new direction.

All this would culminate in the proclamation from the Persian king Darius to rebuild the city and temple at Jerusalem (Ezra 6). In addition, Darius would offer compensation for their expenses and pay to make sure the temple was completed. God would use this ruler to bless and protect the people of Yahweh. Yahweh had already been glorified and would now glorify the people. Haggai used apocalyptic imagery to suggest that the temple was shaken, foreign nations were overturned (had their world rocked by Jerusalem's blessings), and Jerusalem's leaders would be blessed for their faithfulness.

God's Vision of Hope Today

God motivated Jerusalem with a vision of hope, support, power, and encouragement: "The book of Haggai offers a vision of how the use of power can have liberating and creative effects not only for the future of a heap of ruins but also for a community who once knew the pain of exile and the feeling of abandonment by a seemingly disinterested God."[1] The fallen kingdom was able to overcome shame, guilt, fear, and low self-esteem to rebuild their lives. Like many people today, the Israelites had sought help in the wrong people. Help would not come from their government, from themselves, or by focusing on making their lives better. Help came from God, the author of life. The being they offended was the being who wanted relationship with them. The God they ignored was actually the one who could heal their shame. The one whom they avoided was the one who tried to engage them.

First, *God inspires those who are suffering to have hope.* We reach many broken people in Portland who struggle with addictions, pain, fear, anxiety, anger, and regret. However, God is not the enemy. God is the one who wants to be with us, to guide us, and to work with us. Second, *God offers hope in a refurbished life.* The Jerusalem temple, when rebuilt, was much shabbier than the original temple. King Herod rebuilt that shabby second temple to be the glorious Roman structure that Jesus saw when came to clean the sinners out of the court. The temple was majestic, but only because Herod rebuilt it. He rebuilt it because the older temple had been unimpressive. However, God claimed that this rebuilt,

1. Dempsey, *The Prophets*, 130.

unimpressive temple was more glorious than the first. Why? Because it was their temple, not Solomon's. It was a temple built out of hope, love, and vision, not slave labor.

Even more, it was the temple of second chances, renewed hope, and revived relationship. For the returnees to Jerusalem from Babylon, the temple was their new life. In a similar way, for the many we help in recovery at Agape Church of Christ, a restoration of their relationship with God is their new life. Even though people may lose their families, jobs, friendships, businesses, or other things due to an addiction, abuse, or immaturity, recovery promises hope. Recovery doesn't promise that you will come through the process better than you were, but you will come through the promise different, changed, and with a greater appreciation of the things you lost. You will come through with a sense of respect, not shame.

God holds out hope to people that life can begin again. When Jesus was crucified he stated, "It is finished" (John 19:30). In the crucifixion God in Jesus Christ stated, "From this day on I will bless you." The death, burial, and resurrection of Jesus were God's intervention that offered a cleansing agent for our infection, sin, shame, and unclean behavior. As always, God offers intervention, confrontation, and blessing. God knows that we cannot move forward in the relationship if shame, infection, or fear blocks our healing. God, however, offers hope for those overcome with pain. Haggai was the prophet who not only delivered the message, he worked with them. God and the prophet worked with others to build a team that would rebuild the temple and the lives of the people.

"OK Mary," I said. "Please promise me one thing."

"I don't know that I can, pastor," she said.

"I think you can, and I know you can. This is only one thing I want you to promise me. It's the only thing I will ask," I said.

"Why, I know it will be something I can't do," she said, "but I will try."

"You just said it was a God thing I was here. I mentioned to you that your friend told me to visit you because she loved you. I shared with you that I was here because I loved you," I said in my best minister's voice.

"Yes, yes, I know," she said. "What is it? I will do it."

I had been called by someone from the church where Mary had attended for many years. It was a friend, whom I knew, who was concerned about Mary. It was in the small town of Bonne Terre, Missouri, where I served in my first church as a minster. Lori and I had become very involved in the community and knew people in every church. Most of the time we were ministers to our own church. Many times, we were ministers to those in our community—including other churches. It's what happens in a small town; everybody helps each other. There were no reasons to be territorial. The church with an older minister had tremendous resources, wisdom, and history. The church with the younger couple had tremendous energy, young people, and vision. The church with the liberal theologians had cutting-edge ideas. The church with the conservative preacher knew all the verses of the Bible and could apply them in any situation. We all worked together.

Mary had lost Hal, her husband of many years. They had been married for twenty years, then divorced over his infidelity. He remarried twice and so did Mary. During their next marriages they chose partners who shared their passion for alcohol, drugs, and sex. Unfortunately, these relationships opened giant wounds that would never heal. Then, fifteen years later they came back together, attended church, and worked together to raise their granddaughter. They gave their lives back to God and recommitted to each other. The next five years were wonderful. Mary owned a business, and Hal did odd jobs in the community. Mary made a quilt with butterflies on it and Hal carved butterflies. They chose butterflies because butterflies represented a second life that was much prettier than the first. "Butterflies are prettier than worms," Hal would say.

Hal died six months before I met Mary. Hal and Mary focused on mending their relationship rather than on paying their debts. Mary was left with tremendous debt. Hal did everything for her, and she had little clue about finances, taxes, and property values. Mary was devastated.

"Please visit Mary," the friend of hers said to me on the phone. "She told me the other day she would kill herself before filing for bankruptcy."

"Do you believe her?" I asked.

"Yes," her friend said, "I know she will do it. When she sets her mind to something, she does it. She isn't afraid to die; she says it is less painful than living without Hal."

"Mary," I said. "Here is what I am going to ask you. Promise me you will not kill yourself for the next seven days. I am going on vacation tomorrow and I would ask that you wait until I get back. When I return, I would like to talk with you, but please promise me that you will wait till I return. Whatever you do after we meet is up to you." I put my hands out and she grabbed them. I tried to be sneaky and look at her wrists: Whew, no cuts, I thought.

She saw I had looked at her wrists. "Don't worry; pills are my choice..."

PART THREE   Visionaries for Hope

She looked determined and stared into my eyes.

My God, I thought. She's my mom's age . . . I hoped that she would see me as a son who was trying to reach her.

"Okay," she said. "Seven days."

I prayed with her, hugged her, and left. She called out to me, "Have a good vacation, I don't want you to worry. I promise."

She waited. I returned and met with her. Lori and I talked with her, pointed her to a counselor, invited her to church. She joined a small group, and she found help from an accountant. In a small town you work together. Everyone helps each other. You make promises and try to keep them.

She joined us that Christmas for dinner. She had no one else in her family who would take her.

Later she met a man named Robert in one of the grief groups.

They fell in love.

They married.

Every time I would see her, she would cry and say, "Thank you for coming to the shop." She would hug Lori: "Thank you for taking me into your family." Robert would say, "Thank you for going to see her and loving her so I could now love her."

I guess it's one of those wonderful moments, memories, stories that we both share in our years of ministry.

It's a reminder that God can use one visit to change a person's life.

It's also a scary reminder that had I said no to Mary's friend, or had I said, "I'm too busy to visit Mary," she may not be alive, and my family would have missed the opportunity to see God transform another life.

This is why we call Yahweh God in Jesus Christ the God of Second Chances.

Hal was right; butterflies are prettier than worms.

11

Zechariah

Continual Reminders That Develop Hope

I RECEIVED A PHONE call one afternoon at my office.

"Pastor Ron," the voice said on the line, "this is Amy. Can . . . can Steve and I . . . Steve and I need to meet with you and Lori," she nervously said. She sounded concerned, and I began to worry a little. We ministers typically become anxious when someone from our church feels that they need to meet with us immediately.

"Sure Amy," I said. "How about Lori and I come by this afternoon?"

There was a moment's pause. "Uh, okay. Are you sure you want to come by? I know you both are very, very busy and we won't take much of your time."

"It's okay, Amy," I said. "We would be glad to see you both. We haven't visited you since you moved."

"Thank you, thank you, pastor; it won't take much time. Steve and I need to share something with you and Lori."

Steve and Amy were a couple we met at Dignity Village. They had been coming to Agape for about nine months. They were asked to leave the village but found an apartment before they left. We had worried about them being on the streets, as we worry about others who get asked to leave. We also knew that both had a history of addictions and

PART THREE   Visionaries for Hope

drinking. They were welcome at Agape, and Steve started singing on our praise team.

Lori and I took Caleb, our five-year-old, with us to the apartment complex. Steve and Amy were living in a part of Portland close to 82nd Street, a high-prostitution area in southeast Portland. As we entered the apartment building, a woman came out of an apartment next to the entryway. She grabbed her shoes (which were outside the door) and looked at us. As our eyes met a chill went down my spine. It was a feeling of pain, suffering, and evil. Since beginning Agape and working downtown, we have learned to sense places where people suffer— geographical pockets of evil in the community.

"Did you feel that?" Lori said to me.

"Yes, I don't think we will bring our little ones here anymore."

As the woman disappeared down the hall, we headed upstairs to Steve and Amy's apartment. We could sense the pain in this building.

As we entered their apartment Amy and Steve both hugged us. We have always appreciated them and had a good feeling around them. Amy was nervous and asked us to sit down. They went straight to the point. "We love your sermons, pastor, and we like you both. Your lessons on the prophets make us feel good and full of hope," she began. "Last week you said something and we decided that we needed to tell you about us," Steve said.

When I had talked about Zechariah and Haggai, over the past few Sundays, they had heard that God can forgive all that we have done and give us a new start. Steve and Amy began to share their history. Amy was sold to a Latino motorcycle gang at age fifteen for one thousand five hundred dollars. "My life is work fifteen hundred dollars," she said.

Steve's grandmother gave him to a man who took him away and planned to "make a man out of him." Both Amy and Steve experienced drug addiction, sexual and physical abuse, prostitution, and a life of pain. They met years later, married, and began to work together to escape that life. As they shared their story, they ended with their main point. "Both of us are HIV positive and have hepatitis C. We are trying to quit drinking but keep messing up." Lori and I nodded and listened. What they said next brought us to tears.

"Pastor, we should have told you, and now we trust this church and know God loves us. We needed to tell you this. We understand if you won't take us."

"We understand if you won't take us." The words stung both Lori and me. Who, after hearing such a story and having a faith in God, would "not want to take" this couple?

Lori had tears in her eyes and hugged Amy.

"I want to help you with the abuse work you do and the women. I promise if you let me come with you I won't drink that day," Amy cried.

Lori hugged her and said, "If that's what you can do, I am okay with that."

My eyes were welling up with tears as well and I put my hand on Steve's shoulder and said, "Are you kidding? We have been praying for God to lead people like you to Agape. I hope you will take us."

We visited longer. Steve wanted to continue with the praise team, and Amy promised to help in any way she could. They asked us to pray for them, and we asked them to pray for us that we would keep this secret until they were able to share it with their church family. While we were praying, we heard people in the hall yelling, who were drunk, and the woman in the apartment across the hall having sex for money with the man who had hired her. You could hear the pain and suffering in the building, but a feeling of peace pervaded Steve and Amy's apartment.

As Lori and I left with our son, we thought, how could someone *not* want Steve and Amy in their church? We also realized how hard it was for them to live where they were and still believe God would not abandon them. Over the years we developed a great relationship with Steve and Amy. They came to our house for Thanksgiving, were baptized at Christmas, and became involved with some of our ministries. I met their doctor, who is one of the top research specialists with HIV patients, and many of their friends whom they would bring to church. However, life was tough for them. They constantly struggled with guilt, shame, and despair. They, like the Jews who returned from exile, needed constant reminders that God loves them and wanted to hold on to them.

The Struggle of the Ancients to Believe and Hope

Zechariah preached to the Judean exiles who had returned to Jerusalem to rebuild the temple and city. Haggai was his contemporary who began preaching two months previously. The book began in 520 BCE in the eighth month. Zechariah spoke after Haggai had promised the people that God would bless them for rebuilding the temple (Hag 2:1–9).

PART THREE   Visionaries for Hope

Zechariah's messages not only complement Haggai's, but they seem to address the deep-rooted shame that the Judeans must have felt.

In Zech 1:2–6 Yahweh recounted the history of Israel's captivity as well as their repentance. "'Return to me, and I will return to you,' says Yahweh Almighty. Do not be like your ancestors, when the earlier prophets proclaimed: 'This is what Yahweh Almighty says: "Turn from your evil ways and your evil practices."' They would not listen or pay attention to me, declares Yahweh. Where are your ancestors now? Do the prophets live forever? Didn't my words and my decrees, which I commanded my servants the prophets, overcome your ancestors? Then they repented and said, 'Yahweh Almighty has done to us what we deserve, as promised'" (1:2–6). Zechariah went where the people were located. They had been punished, repented, and then were forgiven. The first few chapters of this book heavily addressed the shame and guilt that repentant people face in moving forward. It also displays Yahweh's ability to guide and empower a nation struggling to overcome their shame.

First, *God reinforced love and forgiveness for the people of Judah.* "The angel of Yahweh said, 'Yahweh Almighty, how long will you withhold mercy from Jerusalem and from the towns of Judah, with whom you have been angry these seventy years?' So Yahweh spoke kind and comforting words to the angel who talked with me" (1:12–13). God reminded Zechariah, who reminded the people, that they had been forgiven and would receive mercy. Yahweh promised to bless Jerusalem by living among the nation rebuilding the temple:

> Run, tell that young man, "Jerusalem will be a city without walls because of the great number of people and animals in it. I myself will be a wall of fire around it, and I will be its glory within," declares Yahweh. (Zech 2:5)

> "Shout and be glad, my daughter Zion, because I am coming to live with you," declares Yahweh. (Zech 2:10)

Second, *God chose to forgive the Judeans and made it possible for them to heal.* Zechariah saw a vision where Joshua the high priest was dressed in dirty clothes (an abomination to Yahweh) and was accused/attacked by Satan (Zechariah 3). One can only imagine what Satan was saying! "Your mom's a whore . . . Your dad's a crackhead! "Your family is screwed up. You're lazy, a drunk, a tweeker, a sinner. You disgust me!"

"Worthless."

"Worthless."

Zechariah

"Worthless!"

One can also imagine Joshua's posture: his face red, his heart racing, his fists clenched, and his eyes staring at his own feet. It's a scene we have seen often; some of us have experienced this feeling of shame. Satan is powerful but even more; Satan knows how to enslave us with our own guilt.

Yet Yahweh responded by defending the defiled priest:

> Joshua was dressed in filthy clothes as he stood before the angel. The angel said to those who were standing in front of him, "Take off his filthy clothes." Then he said to Joshua, "See, I have taken away your sin, and I will put fine garments on you." Then I [Zechariah] said, "Put a clean turban on his head." So they put a clean turban on his head and clothed him, while the angel of Yahweh stood by. (Zech 3:4-5)

Even more, Yahweh provided hope for Joshua and his people.

> Listen, High Priest Joshua, you and your associates seated before you, who are men representative of things to come: I am going to bring my servant, the Branch. The stone I have set in front of Joshua, has seven eyes on that one stone, I will engrave an inscription on it, says Yahweh Almighty, and I will remove the sin of this land in a single day. In that day each of you will invite your neighbor to sit under your vine and fig tree, declares Yahweh Almighty. (Zech 3:8-10)

Yahweh's power was displayed in this passage. God would forgive their sins (generations of sins) in a single day. One can imagine Yahweh's excitement (as opposed to the anger of the other prophetic passages) in communicating to Zechariah. Yahweh's passion shone through the shame and guilt that the nation faced. God promised to forgive and cleanse the repentant nation. As in the prophecy of Haggai so also in the book of Zechariah God helped the defiled people gain a new start, because Yahweh knew that unclean people could not become holy by themselves. Therefore, it was up to Yahweh to give them another chance, and to cleanse them so that they could put their past sins behind them. In this vision Yahweh not only gave them a new relationship (removal of the hat and clothes) but empowered their priest to be able to lead them. However, as with all covenants, the condition was still to follow God and keep the commandments. God showed power by "removing the sin of the land in a single day."

PART THREE   Visionaries for Hope

Continual Reminders of Forgiveness

Zechariah saw and reported visions that were highly symbolic to stress to God's people that they were forgiven and in covenant with Yahweh. In Zech 4:6–9 the two olive trees suggested that their leaders were holy and anointed so that they could lead the Judeans closer to God. The flying scroll (5:1–4) illustrated that God's word would continue to purify the people. The woman in the basket carried to Babylon (5:5–11) was a reminder that sin had been left in the great city and therefore forgiven. God's Spirit extended to the scattered peoples in the countries surrounding Jerusalem and promised to lead them back home (6:1–8). Finally, those gathered by the Spirit would come to worship their God at Jerusalem (6:9–15). God gave these many visions to remind the Jews and their leaders that Yahweh cleanses and makes holy. In the past the leaders left God, but in the restoration of the kingdom of God leaders needed to set the pace for the congregation (Ezekiel 34). As leaders obey and are blessed, so the people in turn trust and follow their God. "The people of Bethel had sent Sharezer and Regem-Melek, together with their men, to offer a request to Yahweh by asking the priests of the house of Yahweh Almighty and the prophets, "Should I/we mourn and fast in the fifth month, as I/we have done for so many years?" (Zech 7:2–3).

According to biblical history, God's people continued to worship, celebrate festivals, and observe fasting and prayer while living in sin. The leaders of the people were dishonest and unjust, yet they believed that they were to set an example by following the religious observances God required. However, God stated through the prophets that the leaders of the Jerusalem remnant were called to be just and righteous: "Administer true justice; show mercy and compassion to one another. Do not oppress the widow or the fatherless, the foreigner, or the poor. Do not plan evil against each other" (Zech 7:9–10). Leaders were to focus upon caring for people and treating others with respect, rather than on the worship rituals. While fasting was not bad, it should have been practiced with an honest heart and godly life. For Yahweh a pure heart was manifested by actions and social justice.

Zechariah's audience was challenged to care for others. Fasts were times to humble oneself before their God. However, in the new kingdom God was calling for feasts, not fasts.

> Just as I had determined to bring disaster on you and showed no pity when your ancestors angered me, says Yahweh Almighty, so

> now I have determined to do good again to Jerusalem and Judah. Do not be afraid. These are the things you are to do: Speak the truth to each other, and render true and sound judgment in your courts; do not plan evil against each other, and do not love to swear falsely. I hate all this, declares Yahweh. The word of Yahweh Almighty came to me. This is what Yahweh Almighty says: The fasts of the fourth, fifth, seventh and tenth months will become joyful and glad occasions and happy festivals for Judah. Therefore love truth and peace. (Zech 8:14–19)

While fasting and humility were key elements in the Judean faith, Yahweh encouraged those who had returned to Judah to feast, celebrate, and call all people (including those unclean and Gentiles) to the table of fellowship. The new kingdom was not a kingdom of mourning and fasting. The people had repented, they had been forgiven, and this was the time to feast and celebrate. When we are overcome with shame, we can find many reasons to punish ourselves. However, God wanted the hearers of Zechariah's message to celebrate and feast so that they would forget their shame and fear. In order to lead other peoples to seek Yahweh, God's people needed to know who they were and the hope they had in Yahweh. "In those days ten men from all languages and nations will take firm hold of one Jew by the hem of his robe and say, 'Let us go with you because we have heard that God is with you'" (8:23).

With Visions of Hope Dancing in Their Heads

The next section of the book of Zechariah is divided into two oracles (9:1—11:17; 12:1—14:21). These oracles remind the people that God cares for them. The first oracle announced that God would protect them. God was their king and would fight for them and lead them victoriously in battle against the surrounding kingdoms.

> Rejoice greatly, Daughter Zion! Shout, Daughter Jerusalem! See, your king comes to you, righteous and victorious, lowly and riding on a donkey, on a colt, the foal of a donkey. I will take away the chariots from Ephraim and the warhorses from Jerusalem, and the battle bow will be broken. He will proclaim peace to the nations. His rule will extend from sea to sea and from the River to the ends of the earth. As for you, because of the blood of my covenant with you, I will free your prisoners from the waterless pit. Return to your fortress, you prisoners of hope; even now I

PART THREE   Visionaries for Hope

announce that I will restore twice as much to you. I will bend
Judah as I bend my bow and fill it with Ephraim. (9:9–13)

These were God's people and Yahweh planned to save and protect them. However, their God would deliver peace to them, unlike in the days of the Babylonians. The motivation for this action was the "blood of my covenant with you." Yahweh had restored a relationship with the Jews and promised to bless them: "I will strengthen Judah and save the tribes of Joseph. I will restore them because I have compassion on them. They will be as though I had not rejected them, for I am Yahweh their God and I will answer them" (10:6).

God knew that this people needed to heal from shame and guilt. Therefore, God promised to bless them and stay in relationship. They had been punished in the past because they had violated their covenant/relationship with God: "The flock detested me, and I grew weary of them and said, 'I will not be your shepherd. Let the dying die, and the perishing perish. Let those who are left eat one another's flesh.' Then I took my staff called Favor and broke it, revoking the covenant I had made with all the nations. It was revoked on that day, and so the afflicted of the flock who were watching me knew it was the word of Yahweh" (Zech 11:9–11). Not only was the covenant broken, but Yahweh ended the relationship. It was within God's will to divorce a nation that "detested" the author of their life and well-being. This was not the actions of the people of Zechariah's day; however, they still carried the shame of their parents. Yet God promised to raise up a shepherd who would guide the sheep of Israel and lead them closer to Yahweh (Zech 11:15).

If the first oracle called for rejoicing, the second oracle centered on the protection of the people, Yahweh's punishment on Judah's enemies would involve the restoration of the Jews. Not only would God protect them from their enemies, but they would have their covenant confirmed: "On that day I will set out to destroy all the nations that attack Jerusalem. I will pour out on the house of David and the inhabitants of Jerusalem a spirit of grace and supplication. They will look on me, the one they have pierced, and they will mourn for him as one mourns for an only child, and grieve bitterly for him as one grieves for a firstborn son" (Zech 12:8–10). This outpouring of the Spirit was a symbol for their restoration as a people of God. In addition to this mourning Yahweh reminded them how damaging their rebellion was. While shame was to be removed, guilt would be a reminder that God had been a victim, not the Judeans: "They will call on my name and I will answer them; and will say, "They are my people," and they will say, "Yahweh is our God" (Zech 13:9).

God promised to restore the city and help the nation rebuild as a people holy and loved by their God. The hope of restoration would not only allow healing, it would encourage them to know God's love, honor, and grace.

> On that day living water will flow out from Jerusalem...Yahweh will be king over the whole earth. On that day there will be one Yahweh, and this name the only name. (14:8)

> On that day "holy to Yahweh" will be inscribed on the bells of the horses, and the cooking pots in Yahweh's house will be like the sacred bowls in front of the altar. (Zech 14:20)

Zechariah was a powerful witness to the patience, love, grace, and compassion of God for humans. While many of us at one time believed that the prophets were angry men who raged against the machine, the Hebrew Scriptures indicate that the prophets were sent by God to encourage people. When the Jews returned home from exile, Yahweh knew that their shame could blind them from having hope for the future. Zechariah, however, provides hope for those in shame, guilt, sin, and bondage. The repeated messages of forgiveness and hope needed to happen because the repeated messages of sin and disobedience lay before their eyes. Rebuilding a temple that one caused to be destroyed, remodeling a city flattened by the sins of your family, and rekindling a relationship with a God hurt by the nation would have brought painful reminders to the Jews of their history of sin. However, Zechariah called the people to trust and believe that Yahweh could and would forgive.

Breaking Free by Breaking Shame

Rodney came to Agape one Sunday morning. He had been invited by one of our members to attend worship before Christmas. He had been living on the streets and struggled with heroin addiction. When he came to Agape, he was living in a transitional shelter waiting to receive government-subsidized housing and attending a recovery group. After the sermon he came to me and said, "I might be back." That was in 2008. Within two months Rodney had his own apartment, took a job at Subway, began to lead our sexual-addictions recovery group, sang on our praise

PART THREE   Visionaries for Hope

team, helped with our downtown outreach, and was a regular on Sunday mornings. However, in spite of all this, he struggles with shame. His abuse as a child impacted his view of reality, God, and people.

As an outstanding athlete in college, an army veteran, and former worship leader in a Pentecostal church, Rodney masked the pain as well as his addictions (an attempt to kill the pain) for years. After hitting rock bottom, he decided to give God another try. However, many of our conversations involved convincing him that God could love him. No matter what he read, heard, and sang, he struggled to believe that God was with him. He needed a church community and band of brothers in a group to remind him how far he had come and how God would not let him go. I have come to realize in my time with Rodney that shame has such a hold on people that even believing in God's unconditional love and grace was difficult. Those in shame not only wrestle with guilt; they wrestle with God. They, like the returning Judeans, need constant reminders that God cares and loves them.

Zechariah not only reminded his audience that they were forgiven. He called them to feast and celebrate life in God. Life as a new kingdom was not designed to be a time of mourning. It was designed to be vibrant and a passionate experience of life. It was also designed to be a response to shame, not a partner with it.

Those of us who have been called to preach are reminded by prophets such as Haggai, Zechariah, Joel, and Ezekiel that it takes more positive comments and illustrations than negative ones to move people closer to God. The book of Zechariah, for example, contains many illustrations of forgiveness, grace, hope, and mercy. God knew that people need to be reminded that they have been forgiven. God also knew that people need to be reminded that they have hope. Our energies can best be spent reminding others of the hope within them than reminding them that they have failed.

Most people don't need reminders of failure. They face the truth daily. Whether we experience this truth on the news media, at work, in our neighborhoods, in our families, or as we go out in public we are reminded:

- Humans fail.
- We fail.
- Others fail.
- God is perfect.

This is why we need constant reminders that:

- God forgives.
- God has forgiven.
- God will forgive.
- God wants us to believe we are forgiven.

PART FOUR

Calling for Hope

12

Malachi

Confronting Those Who Destroy Hope

"Congratulations," I said to Karen one Sunday morning. She seemed puzzled and looked down at the floor. "Congratulations!" I smiled and said again. "You are free."

She still seemed confused, and said, "I'm sorry, I don't understand."

Her daughter and son glanced at her and then me curiously. I then thought to myself that maybe I wasn't supposed to say anything and that she was embarrassed. For many years my wife, Lori, has led a spiritual support group for women in abusive relationships or for survivors of abuse. We have witnessed the courage and strength many of these women have displayed in leaving their abusive husbands and healing in their walk with Jesus. While much of what happens in the group is confidential, I have been allowed to talk with and celebrate with these women as they become stronger in their self-esteem and healing. Karen was one of these women we have both prayed with about the struggle to be loved and honored as any woman in relationship deserves to be.

"Karen," I said, "Congratulations, you are free. You left your abusive husband and that requires great faith and strength. It's his own fault for not repenting and changing his behavior. We are very happy for you, and God is proud of you."

She and the children looked shocked. Then tears began to well up in her eyes. "I—I don't know what to say."

"You've never been told that before, have you? You haven't heard that God approves of someone leaving their abuser and getting a divorce, have you?"

She shook her head no while tears continued to form in her eyes. I realized how hard this must have been for her and her children. I began to tell her why most churches don't address domestic violence: because they do not believe that divorce is an option. Lori and I have had this discussion with many women, with male clergy, with other Christian leaders, and with abusive and controlling males. They all admit that abuse is wrong (or at least they suggest it is not a good thing). Sometimes we can get them to admit that abuse is a sin and something God hates. However, few will admit that divorce is acceptable when a spouse violates the covenant through violence, verbal humiliation, neglect, sin, pornography, or dysfunction.

Does God Hate Divorced People?

I have heard countless sermons proclaiming the evils of divorce, declaring how easily the world ends marriages, and announcing that there is no good reason for divorce. Even though Jesus gave permission for divorce in cases of sexual infidelity (which would include many sexual sins—Matt 19:1–10; Mark 10:1–17), preachers continue to tell the victims that they are bound until the death of their spouse. Even though the Apostle Paul gave permission to send an unbelieving spouse (including a spouse who practices unbelieving behavior) out the door, we Christians have hesitated to allow people freedom to leave a marriage where one person brings sin and destructive behavior into the relationship (1 Cor 7:12–16).[1] While statistics suggest that children suffer from divorce and that those in single-female-parent homes are at risk, few people are willing to address the emotional damage that occurs when a woman stays in a relationship with an abusive or dysfunctional spouse, or with one who continues in addictive behavior.

Malachi 2:14 has become the battle cry for those opposing divorce. In the New Revised Standard Version, it reads in part as follows: "Because the LORD was a witness between you and the wife of your youth, to whom

---

1. For more on Paul's explanation of marriage to those in dysfunction see my book, *The Better Way*, 72–77.

you have been faithless, though she is your companion and your wife by covenant" (NRSV). However, this is a grossly misused, misquoted, and misapplied Bible verse. Many, especially clergy and abusers, have used this text to tell victims that God does not approve of divorce. Therefore, victims have no other option but to stay in the relationship, accept the abuse, and hope for change. The text seems to be difficult to reconcile if we take the view that God is opposed to any divorce. But is the text meant to enslave spouses in violent relationships? One woman we worked with, whose husband returned to alcohol abuse and the neglect of his family shared with me that she had told him, if he continued to do this, he was out. Her husband replied, "So you're quitting on this marriage?" When she shared this with one of our ministers and me, we reminded her that her husband had quit the marriage by his actions. Victims should never be blamed for the dysfunction in a relationship. Those in sin should accept responsibility, repent for their actions, and make amends to those they have hurt.

Hope Destroyed through Broken Relationships

The setting of the book of Malachi suggests that the people of Judah had returned from captivity. As time passed, they also returned to the ways of their former generations by neglecting the sacrifices and practicing idolatry.

> I have loved you, says Yahweh. But you ask, "How have you loved us?" Wasn't Esau Jacob's brother? declares Yahweh. Yet I have loved Jacob, and hated Esau, yet I have turned his hill country into a wasteland and left his inheritance to the desert jackals. A son honors his father, and a slave his master. If I am a father, where is the honor I should receive? If I am a master, shouldn't I be respected? says Yahweh Almighty. Priests, you show contempt for my name. But you ask, "How have we shown contempt for your name?" By offering defiled food on my altar. But you ask, "How have we defiled you?" When you say that Yahweh's table is contemptible and offer blind animals for sacrifice, is that not wrong? When you sacrifice lame or diseased animals, is that not wrong? Try offering them to your governor! Would he be pleased with you? Would he accept you? says Yahweh Almighty. (Mal 1:2–6)

PART FOUR   Calling for Hope

While Yahweh was the offended husband in the prophetic book of Hosea, Yahweh became the offended wife in Mal 2:11–16.[2] Israel had married a foreigner and had begun to practice injustice which was the same behavior that caused the previous divorce. How was God to respond to this behavior? "Judah has acted treacherously, or faithlessly, and committed an abomination in Israel and Jerusalem. Judah profaned what was holy to Yahweh by loving a foreign god's daughter" (Mal 2:11).

Yahweh entered a dialogue with the leaders of Israel, through the prophet Malachi, and suggested that they were trying to deflect responsibility for their sin.

- I have loved you . . . , but you ask, "How have you loved us?" (1:1)
- You ask, "How have we shown contempt for your name?" (1:6)
- You place defiled food on my altar, but you ask, "How have we defiled you?" (1:7)
- You have wearied Yahweh with your words. "How have we wearied Yahweh?" you ask. (2:4)
- Return to me and I will return to you . . . But you ask, "How shall we return?" (2:7)
- You rip me off, but you ask, "How do we rip you off?" (2:8)
- You have said harsh things against me . . . Yet you ask, "What have we said against you?" (2:13)

In this question-and-answer session Yahweh convicted Judah of neglect, abuse, and failure to uphold their covenant with God. Dempsey suggests that major themes of this book involve God's love, honor, justice, and the faithfulness and repentance of the people of Judah.[3] However Judah was again rejecting God's love and faithfulness. Yahweh protected them and punished Edom for refusing to show compassion (Mal 1:4–5; Obad 1–8). God sought Judah's best interest and became vulnerable by seeking relationship and blessing them (Jer 33:31–34). Yet Judah returned to their old ways and neglected their God by offering leftovers, allowing violent and evil people to be blessed, and refusing to believe that God's values of truth, faith, honesty, and grace were honorable. They once again turned

---

2. For texts that portray God as mother/wife/female see Isa 42:14; 46:3; 66:9–13. While John 4 suggests that God is spirit, the Scriptures as a whole present both masculine and feminine imagery for God. See Smith, *The Origins of Biblical Monotheism*, 90.

3. Dempsey, *The Prophets*, 139.

their head to violence and rejected faithfulness and loyalty to their God. As with Jeremiah and Hosea, God became a vulnerable, hurt, and victimized spouse who accepted unfaithful Judah. Judah was allowed to come home but returned to their controlling, abusive, and neglectful behavior. To say that they relapsed was an understatement. Judah also blamed God for being oversensitive by arguing and questioning the Creator of the world who knew all things. In Judah's mind God was "quitting the marriage"; however, God reminded the covenant partner that they were truly at fault. The Persian ruler demanded obedience and respect which they would have given, as a colonized community. Yet they neglected the king of creation to whom the people who owed their salvation and lives.

First, *God had earlier practiced divorce against those who profaned the holy covenant* (Isa 50:1; 54:6–7; Jer 3:8). As we discussed earlier, God was the offended spouse in a dysfunctional marriage. While covenant was meant to be holy, pure, loving, and safe; Israel had sinned and hurt faithful Yahweh. The Babylonian captivity was a time that Yahweh had "kicked out" the offender to teach that relationships involved honor, trust, respect, and faithfulness. After seventy years of couch surfing, living on the streets, and limited visitation, Judah (or at least some of the key leaders) had repented. Yahweh opened the doors to the home and began to rebuild the marriage. Yahweh had a reputation of holding the spouse accountable for their contribution to the marriage. In Ezra 10:11, Ezra and the Jewish leaders encouraged men who were married to foreign women to divorce their foreign wives. If Mal 2:11 suggests that the Judean men may have been married to foreign wives, then what are the implications of this text?[4] In Mal 2:16 God was displeased with divorce. However, this does not mean that God was not willing to practice it.

Second, *the Malachi text does not discuss literal marriages but applies to holiness and faithfulness in covenant.*[5] The term for covenant was used throughout Malachi to refer to Judah's relationship with Yahweh.

- I have loved you (1:2)
- Warning about breaking the *covenant* with Levi (2:4)

---

4. Mal 2:11 states, "Judah has married the daughter of a foreign god." This can have two interpretations. First, the text can suggest that the Jewish men were married to foreign women. Second, the text can mean that the Jewish nation is again involved in idolatry. Biblical scholars support both interpretations.

5. For further discussion on this in the context of marriage, abuse, and divorce; and to find resources over viewing the controversial interpretations surrounding this verse, see Clark, *Setting the Captives Free*, 65–69.

PART FOUR Calling for Hope

- *Covenant* of life and peace, Levi respected me (2:5)
- You have turned from me (2:8)
- Why do you profane my *covenant*? (2:10)
- Judah has *broken faith* and married the daughter of a foreign god (2:11)
- The Lord will cut him (Judah) off (2:12)
- False tears, remember the wife of your youth (Yahweh); and b*roken faith* with your wife (Yahweh) (2:14)
- One God made them both (2:10)
- I hate divorce so *do not break faith* (2:16)

These texts indicate that the Judeans were dishonoring their master, father, and wife. The wife of their youth was to be *Yahweh*. Judah had left *Yahweh* and cleaved to another woman or god (probably the goddess Asherah, which was worshiped by the Judeans, according to Jeremiah 44). Yahweh challenged Judah in court, like an angry, hurt wife, and warned them that they were about to divorce—something God did not wish to do. The final statement was, "Guard yourself in your spirit and *do not break faith*" or "It's either her or me!" (Mal 2:15b). This interpretation is more in line with God's view of divorce (an aggressive action to protect the sanctity of covenant), but it does not suggest that God will not allow divorce.

Finally, the text continues to teach that *God will not tolerate violence or sin in the covenant relationship*. "I hate divorce," says Yahweh the God of Israel, "and one clothing/covering themselves with violence/lawlessness," says Yahweh Almighty, "so guard yourself in your spirit, and do not break faith." While God may not wish to divorce the people, God equally hates violent/lawless individuals. Malachi indicated that the Judeans were showing partiality in the law (2:9), committing injustices (2:17), oppressing the poor (3:5), and practicing evil (3:15). In my work with abusers and survivors, the first part of this text is commonly used to control victims and promote the notion that God is angry with wives for leaving, divorcing, and filing a restraining order. Few, however, admit that God is angry with them for their violence, controlling behavior, and oppression. The literal translation can be, "I hate the man who covers himself [a sexual metaphor] with violence," which can also suggest sexual abuse. While God hates divorce, the Creator will practice it in order to keep victims free from violence, oppression, and injustice. The text suggests that those who hurt or oppress their spouses are against God, not those seeking refuge and safety from oppression.

Malachi 2:16 does not suggest that God is angry with divorced people. The text also does not say that people cannot divorce their spouses. The text warns those who are unfaithful *and violent* in their relationships with Yahweh and *other humans*. Since *Yahweh* calls for relationships to promote peace, respect, and honor for both parties; Malachi notes that drastic actions sometimes have to happen to protect and honor covenant relationships. The text also reminds us that people many times return to their former patterns of behavior and need intervention.

Malachi does, however, provide strength for those in marriages where one partner is abusive, neglectful, and unwilling to take responsibility for problem behavior. The seven questions in Malachi suggest that Judah's foolishness and arrogance were manifested by attempts to hide sin from Yahweh. God even accused them of rebellion (3:13). They had become so hardened that they believed that those who were evil were good role models.

In marriage counseling sessions I have been present to confront a male who has violated his marriage vows through abuse, addictive behaviors, neglect, sexual infidelity, pornography, or habitual dishonesty. Typically he responds by justifying his behavior. Sometimes he acts as if he "doesn't know what you are talking about," or "wonders why you would think this of me." Other times he fires questions at us, blaming others for being judgmental, unsympathetic, or guilty of sin ourselves. At times he justifies his behavior by becoming hostile and confrontational. I am sometimes called a feminist or male basher. I am told at times that I am too judgmental or that "we all sin, and you need to lighten up." However, we need to be mature about our sin. When confronted we must repent and do the difficult work to change, which is the true measure of our courage. Rarely have I seen a time when the male admits sin and, like King David, confesses to the group. It does happen, but not often. Our response to confrontation concerning our sin determines what type of spouse we are. As men we need to "man up," which means to "grow up" and act adult about our issues.

The people of Judah, like the majority of these men, resisted Yahweh's probing questions and tried to justify returning to "the sins of their former generations." Malachi was sent to prepare the way for God's intervention in their lives and to call them to repentance. They had been

PART FOUR   Calling for Hope

accepted by Yahweh, but were turning back to their other lovers. They needed to grow up and accept responsibility.

Yet, during this flagrant display of rebellion, sin, and rejection Yahweh offered hope. First, *God's desire was for the name of Yahweh to be respected and honored throughout the world.* God wanted praise from those in other countries.

> "You will see it with your own eyes and say, 'Great is Yahweh—even beyond the borders of Israel.'" (Mal 1:5)
>
> "My name will be great among the nations, from the rising to the setting of the sun. In every place incense and pure offerings will be brought to my name, because my name will be great among the nations..." (1:11)
>
> "For I am a great king... and my name is to be respected among the nations." (1:14)

One can almost envision Malachi's smile as he proclaims God's belief, God's faith, and God's hope to be respected and honored. Like a woman married to a cruel man, who dreams of the day her husband will honor her around her friends and family, so Yahweh seeks to be honored by those created in the divine image. It was not too much for God to ask to be treated with respect. This language was also common propaganda for Darius, the Persian king. If the people could honor their earthly king, how much more should they honor their heavenly king?

Second, *God wanted them to change so that they could be blessed in their relationship.* Yahweh reminded the nation that they were loved. The remaining questions were God's call to repentance so that they could be faithful in their relationship with their Lord. While Judah had mistreated and turned on their God, hope was still offered to them.

Some Rekindle Hope When They Embrace God

"Those who feared Yahweh talked with each other, and Yahweh listened and heard. A scroll of remembrance was written in his presence concerning those who feared Yahweh and honored his name. 'On the day when I act,' says Yahweh Almighty, 'they will be my treasured possession. I will spare them, just as a father has compassion and spares his son who serves him. You will again see the distinction between the righteous and the wicked, between those who serve God and those who do not'" (Mal 3:16-18). A group of God's people was moved to respond and please God. Malachi's words touched their hearts and motivated them to change. God listened to them and promised to again protect a remnant and bless those who were faithful. They would be spared. Yahweh was planning an intervention. One intervention involved blessing; the other involved judgment—although this one would come through a messenger who would prepare the way for Yahweh: "See, I will send the prophet Elijah to you before that great and dreadful day of Yahweh comes. He will turn the hearts of the parents to their children, and the hearts of the children to their parents; or else I will come and strike the land with total destruction" (Mal 4:5-6). God's intervention would involve blessing and judgment. The judgment would involve, as it always had, a prophet who warned people. As in the past, God would not completely destroy the good and bad in judgment. The prophet would preach to draw out a remnant who would turn to Yahweh, receive protection, and overcome the wicked. The evil would suffer for their sin.

Malachi 4:5-6 tells us that Yahweh sends people to warn, encourage, and call others to return to their God. This is "preparing the way" for Yahweh to visit them. In this call some drew closer to God while others justified their sin, rebellion, and dysfunction in their covenant with their Lord. However, God is faithful in sending guides and advisors.

The prophet's call would turn the hearts of children and parents toward each other. This healing within the family would provide hope for the future as the adults would act out of compassion and justice toward the vulnerable of society. This care for the vulnerable had been lacking in Judah. The Greek version of the text, set down near 160 BCE, is slightly different. It states, "He will turn the hearts of the fathers to their sons and people toward their neighbor." This message of hope during the Greek occupation of Palestine was that God hoped for a time when the Jewish people would reach out to their neighbors in justice and compassion. The prophet sent by Yahweh would call the nation to reach out in compassion and peace.

These same words were uttered decades later by God's angel (*malachi*, in Hebrew) to Zechariah the priest concerning his son John (known as John the Baptist). "He will go on before the Lord, in the spirit and power of Elijah, to turn the hearts of the parents to their children and the disobedient to the wisdom of the righteous—to make ready a people prepared for the Lord" (Luke 1:17). Preparing people for the coming of Jesus involved the righteous remnant teaching and turning others to

God's wisdom. As John's father Zechariah later said, John was going to teach salvation through forgiveness of sins. This would be due to God's mercy: "You, my child, will be called a prophet of the Most High; for you will go on before the Lord to prepare the way for him, to give his people the knowledge of salvation through the forgiveness of their sins, because of the tender mercy of our God" (Luke 1:76–78).

But Malachi 3 is more than just a prophecy of Jesus and John the Baptist. It suggests that the prophets play an important role in the visitation of God and the salvation of people. John, like Elijah, Malachi, and the other prophets, was sent to call people back to their God. This preaching helped to separate those who needed a chance to change from those who justified their sin by attacking God, the prophets, and those calling for holiness. While John and Jesus fulfilled this prophecy of Malachi, the meaning of the prophecy did not end with them.

As we will discuss in the following chapter, the church continues the role of the prophets and of John the Baptist. In order for Jesus to enter people's lives and communities, someone must be sent to preach. That preaching is more than simply words or a well-crafted sermon. The prophetic message must be an engagement in the community—engagement that seeks to call those who will listen and return to the Lord with their hearts. It seeks those who will turn their hearts to their children, parents, neighbors, and the wisdom of the righteous. This happens when the church fully engages it's community through love, mercy, and compassion.

Missional and Incarnational Movements

The Dead Sea Scrolls community reread the prophets as if they were speaking in their time and to their community.[6] They saw themselves as the chosen ones of God who were called to bring back the Torah (Law of Moses) and purify the nation. However, they withdrew from their communities and tried to "avoid the sin of a corrupt world." Today many churches try to follow this model of retreating from "the world." The missional movements that have helped to revive the Christian communities in our world do not believe that retreating, hiding, or withdrawing from community is a calling from Jesus. While the prophets can be used today to empower the remnant to return to God and restore the kingdom, Malachi challenges us to engage our community, to call people back to

---

6. Lorein, "The Holy Spirit at Qumran," 395.

Malachi

God, to restore the empire of Jesus, and confront those who destroy hope in our world today. We, as Malachi and the promised Elijah, can prepare people to meet Jesus.

Applying the end of the Malachi prophecy to John the Baptist (in the gospels) and the coming of Jesus, who was to be Yahweh in the flesh, provides a challenge for the church today. Jesus would bring God's justice to protect those who were faithful and judge those who would not listen. In Malachi's day people were again violating their relationship with Yahweh. As in Jeremiah God was threatening divorce. Only this time Yahweh was not planning to hire a divorce lawyer to mediate; Yahweh was going to deal with the issue in person. However, a prophet (like Malachi) would be sent to warn people to turn to God. Yahweh claimed that the prophet would turn parents and children to each other so that the land would be spared. As the faith of the nation affected the land as well, so the faith of a family reflects the heart of the people.

The Greek version of this prophetic text states that the fathers' hearts would return to the sons and the human to their neighbor. The angel told Zechariah, John the Baptist's father, that John would fulfill this by turning the fathers' hearts to their sons, and the mind of the righteous to prepare for the Lord. The consistent phrase concerns the fathers' need to be challenged to love their children. Malachi's prophecy was a call to a people beginning to ignore their God.

Malachi's calling was to turn people, especially fathers, back to God and others. In a time when males struggle to attend church, to commit themselves to a discipleship relationship with Jesus, and live in opposition to our culture's teachings concerning masculinity, Malachi reminds males that the work begins with us.

The gospels illustrated the struggles males have to maintain compassion. For example, in Matthew 1, when Joseph heard that Mary was pregnant by someone other than himself, Joseph struggled to believe and accept Mary. Yet Matthew reminds us that Joseph was a "righteous man and did not want to expose her [Mary] to public humiliation" (Matt 1:19). In Joseph's world a righteous man followed the law and punished without mercy. However, Matthew is suggesting that a new "righteous man" emerges with the coming of Jesus. Righteousness in Matthew's gospel entails grace, mercy, and compassion. This is evident as Jesus calls the disciples to practice righteousness greater than the righteousness of the religious leaders by respecting and valuing other people, especially vulnerable others (Matthew 5–7). The religious leaders even miss the important concepts of the law: justice, mercy, and faithfulness (Matt 23:23). This gospel teaches that the righteous ones of Jesus are those who perform acts of mercy and compassion for the "least of these" (Matt 25:37). In the ancient world justice and righteousness involved social justice and acts of charity. For Matthew the restoration of the kingdom began with a father (Joseph) who acted out of the new righteousness of Christianity.

Luke's gospel also teaches that salvation began with those who showed compassion. Zechariah was rebuked for his faithlessness while Mary was blessed by her willingness to believe (Luke 1:18, 38). The shepherds, who were considered outcasts, were the first ones to see the newborn messiah (Luke 2:1–18). Jesus's ministry in Luke was characterized by his compassionate attention to the poor and marginalized people.

Mark's gospel began in a similar fashion to ancient Roman histories and calendars in praise of Caesar Augustus. In the beginning of Mark Jesus was the new emperor who called his band of men to quickly grow and spread the report that Jesus was king (Mark 1:1). This king enacted peace rather than war and violence. John also began his gospel with John the Baptist's act of submission, testimony, and support for Jesus; however, it began with men. While women have for centuries been great examples of our faith, males have consistently struggled to be like Jesus. The gospel writers not only believed that Jesus was the manifestation of the Day of Yahweh; they knew that Jesus had come to turn human hearts toward one another. The Day of Yahweh was not only a day of punishment; it was a day of mercy.

Confronting Ourselves So That We Might Offer Hope

As I was hurrying into the post office, the usual Portland winter rain made all those heading for the door quicken their steps. Twenty feet from the door, a person sat in a wheelchair, dressed in black, heavily clothed, with a hood pulled tightly. As I came closer to the door, I noticed that those exiting avoided making eye contact with the wheelchair user. Some would shake their heads as they hurried to their cars. I hated going to this post-office branch because I knew it was the slowest branch in Portland, and I was in a hurry. I definitely did not need to stop and slow down today.

As I passed the wheelchair, I heard a female voice asking those leaving for spare change. I knew what would happen when I left. She would ask for money, the Holy Spirit would thump me and expect me to display God's compassion, and I would then struggle with whether or not I would be obedient to the call of Jesus. As I came back out of the post office, I decided that this was the day of selfishness, disobedience, and acting as if I were too busy to hear God's voice. I made a choice. I ducked my head as I came out the door, but somehow my eyes met her eyes.

She said, "Do you have any spare change?"

Well, I thought, I can't very well ignore her since many of my friends have told me how they have felt when people walk by them and ignore their pleas for spare change. I figured I could give some form of obedience to God by acting interested and looking her in the eyes. "No ma'am," I said, smiling. "I'm sorry but I don't have anything. Have a good day." She smiled, "Thanks anyway; have a good day too."

As I grabbed the door handle to my truck, it hit me, or I should say the Spirit hit me. I had forgotten that I had a dollar in my wallet. I returned to the woman in the chair as two others passed her, but as I came closer I thought, Melody?

I stood a few feet from in front of her chair and said, "I'm sorry. I lied to you. I have a dollar left and I can give that to you." Then I said, "Melody, is that you?"

She looked up and smiled, "Yes, pastor, it's me. I thought I recognized you. I didn't think you recognized me."

"I do now," I said. "What happened?"

Melody had come to Agape many years before. She was close friends with a couple who were part of our core group of fifteen who began Agape. These friends were both professors at one of Portland's universities. Melody, her husband, and their two children had begun to deal with marriage issues, and our friends (the professors) brought them to Agape. Melody continued with us for a few weeks, even as she and her husband broke up. Then she left town, and her husband moved back to his family's home in another state. Outside the post office that day, Melody told me that since she had seen us at Agape, she had turned back to meth, and because of her abuse of the drug had become very sick and now paralyzed.

Geez, I thought. It's only been a year!

Melody was in a treatment center nearby and not doing well. She shared how much she missed us, the church, and the life she'd had. I mentioned to her our recovery group that met in that neighborhood, and that we would love to see her again. "You know you are always welcome with us," I said.

PART FOUR Calling for Hope

She cried. "Thank you. I know. I hope I can come some day."

After a few more moments of talking about our families, I left. The rain was a little heavier now and I walked a little more slowly. Melody stayed at her post in the rain and continued to ask for alms. People walked by and hurried on to their vehicles.

I was one of them who hurried.

I know that God was hammering my heart to get me to respond.

As I sat in my truck, it took me a few minutes to get it started. I was overwhelmed with emotion so I sat there for five minutes. Once again I had almost missed a chance to engage someone who was hurting from sin. Once again I had almost succeeded in hardening my heart to the Spirit's guidance. Once again I'd almost turned off the be-like-Jesus switch in my life. Once again the temple doors had almost shut, nearly hiding God's glory from the people. Even more, once again my heart hurt for a human we knew and loved, who had taken the wrong path.

I realized how quickly sin can wreck lives, relationships, and families. It doesn't take long. This is why we need compassion, and why we must confront those who destroy hope in others. This is also why we must confront ourselves when we resist compassion. Preparing the way for Jesus calls for compassion.

13

Jesus, the God of Second Chances

Incarnation at Subway

I HAD MET PHILIP at church one Sunday. He was living on the street and struggling to overcome a drug habit. I hadn't seen him for a few weeks and was worried about him. I finally was able to connect with him downtown under the Burnside Bridge where he was hiding from the rain. He had Andrew with him. While Philip had agreed to meet with me, he must have forgotten and seemed to be hiding from me. As I talked with him Andrew listened.

"Let's go to get something to eat," I said. "I'm buying."

We headed for the Subway where Roger, one of our Agape members who had been on the streets, worked. Andrew had told me he was in a sexually abusive relationship with another male. He decided to take his chances on the streets with his addiction and prostitution rather than to live with a man who beat him and then tried to ask forgiveness with "make-up sex," as he put it.

As Philip, Andrew, and I sat down to eat our "five-dollar foot-long" sandwiches, we began to talk about their lives. Philip had been clean three weeks and we celebrated that victory. Andrew felt that God was punishing him because he was gay, and that his partner was justified in his violence.

"Andrew," I quietly said, "love is not violent. No one has the right to abuse another person, no matter who they are. Sex is not taken; it is shared."

"Is God punishing me?" he asked.

"No, your friend is violating you," I said. "God is love and that is something we need to talk more about."

Philip changed the subject. He had a church background and wanted to talk church. He had pushed Andrew to come to Agape but now wanted to talk about "right" religion.

"Pastor," he asked, "Are Muslims right in their religion?" Andrew had his head down when Philip mentioned this, so I assumed this had been an ongoing discussion.

"It's not about who is right or not. I think it has to do with who Jesus is."

They both nodded their heads.

I continued by quoting the Koran: "Allah is only one God: far be it from His glory that He should have a son" (*Surah* 4:171). Our differences, I said, do not concern our worship of God/Allah/Yahweh, but who we believe Jesus to be. Christians believe that Jesus is God in the flesh. This is difficult for Muslims because Allah is distant and to be worshiped. Jesus, however, is God among us.

I shared with Philip and Andrew how Jesus ate with people, lived among them, hung out with "sinners," and became their friends. This is too difficult for some to believe, but it is the foundation of Christianity. In addition to this, God's incarnation in Jesus is something to be imitated rather than taught.

"So, if I understand you correctly," Andrew followed up, "he ate with common people and hung out with them."

Philip put his sandwich down and said, "Yeah, like we are doing now. Right, pastor?"

"Yeah," I said, "and my job is to do the same because I want to be like Jesus and I need to set an example for my church."

I took another bite. "Oh yeah, and because I love you guys . . ."

They both laughed. "Yeah, right. Whatever." We went back to eating and visiting.

Living among the Exiles: Hoping for Restoration

Christian scholars speak often of the "incarnation." This is a Latin word which means that God became flesh. However, while we understand that God became flesh, we struggle to believe that in becoming flesh/human God (in Jesus) became like us. Jesus lived in a normal house in Judah, had

Jesus, the God of Second Chances

a normal job, worked with his father (who was a construction worker/builder), and became friends with average people. His friendships were not among the elite, the highly educated, or the political leaders of his day. His friends were common fishermen, accountants/moneylenders, farmers, and marginalized people. Jesus, like the prophets of old, lived among the people who were in exile. He was labeled the friend of sinners and tax collectors, which indicates that he developed relationships among the lower classes (Matt 11:19; Luke 7:34).

The Roman government ruled the known world and had become the colonizers. Caesar Augustus was considered a lord, a god, and the author of salvation. His name was powerful, and so were those of succeeding Caesars. Jesus, the true king, and his followers claimed the same titles used by Caesar and his followers; however Jesus was not a warrior, political ruler, or violent man. Jesus was a captive among the captives, a colonized man among the colonies, and a servant among the masses. Yet the Gospels continually remind us that he, like Yahweh, was the God of second chances. He brought true peace (*shalom*) to people and their communities.

The Shalom of Jesus and Restoration

The Judeans were an occupied country in the first century. They looked for restoration, healing, and the reestablishment of their kingdom once again. Luke emphasizes this in two passages. First, when Jesus was born and brought to be circumcised, Luke wrote that Simon was "waiting for the comfort of Israel . . ." (2:29). This language sounds similar to words in the book of Isaiah (40:1). (Anna was also present that day, and shared Jesus with others who were "looking forward to the redemption of Jerusalem," Luke 2:38.) Second, in the book of Acts (also authored by Luke), the apostles ask Jesus if he had come to "restore the empire to Israel" (1:6). So in the gospels and Acts one will read that the Jews hoped for their kingdom to be restored. As with the return from Babylon and rebuilding Jerusalem, the Jews under Roman rule longed for the kingdom to be reestablished. The restoration of the kingdom of God would bring hope and peace for those resisting the oppression.

First, *John the Baptist's appearance at the beginning of the gospels fulfilled the role of Elijah, prophesied in Malachi 4*. Isaiah's prophecy was also used in the gospels to suggest that John was the one who prepared the way for Jesus/God to come to the people: "A voice of one calling In

PART FOUR Calling for Hope

the wilderness, 'Prepare the way for Yahweh; make straight in the desert a highway for our God'" (Isa 40:3). John's emphasis on repentance and baptism, and his appearance as Elijah the prophet, indicated that his role was to prepare the way for Jesus. This Jesus was God leading the captives home from the East (Matthew 3; Mark 1; Luke 3). In John 1 the Baptist refused to acknowledge that he was Elijah but focused on preparing people for the return of God who was coming to turn them to the kingdom.

Jesus was God living among the people to both judge the wicked and rescue the faithful. So Jesus confronted the Pharisees and other religious leaders, thereby taking honor from them and gaining respect in his community. Jesus embraced the suffering and the little ones in his community. He lived among the homeless, prostitutes, tax collectors, common workers, and everyday people. Jesus was marginalized to redeem the marginalized. Jesus, like the prophets of old, left the council of Yahweh to connect with the captives and free the oppressed (Luke 4:16–19).

Second, *the language of Jesus's baptism suggests that Jesus was Yahweh's son who came to restore God's empire.* John the Baptist claimed that Jesus would baptize with the Spirit and fire. These images of the Spirit and fire are also found in the prophetic books. Yahweh poured out fire or wrath on the wicked, and poured out the Spirit on those seeking salvation: "I baptize you with water for repentance. After me comes one who is more powerful than I, whose sandals I am not worthy to carry. He will baptize you with the Holy Spirit and fire. His winnowing fork is in his hand, and he will clear his threshing floor, gathering his wheat into the barn and burning up the chaff with fire" (Matt 3:11–12). Jesus, like Yahweh, would be the judge of all. In addition to this, Jesus would bring people into relationship through the Spirit. The pouring out or baptism of the Spirit was a metaphor for restoration, reconciliation, and reunion with God. Jesus would punish the wicked and restore those who sought God through the Spirit.

In Mark 1:10 after Jesus was baptized, the sky was torn open and the Spirit descended on Jesus. The "ripping of the heavens" was apocalyptic imagery for the coming of a deity or for intervention and the Day of Yahweh. Jesus was God ripping open the heavens and coming to earth. In Jesus's baptism the Day of Yahweh was presented to the people while God testified that Jesus was the chosen Son. That Day was also manifested through Jesus's miracles, causing people to exclaim that God had visited them (Luke 7:16).

Jesus, the God of Second Chances

Jesus represented both Yahweh and the Judean people as he fulfilled Scripture. Throughout the Gospel of Matthew Jesus completed the Scriptures, again suggesting that he, unlike ancient Israel, modeled faithfulness to Yahweh. Matthew's use of words from Isaiah and Zechariah suggested that Jesus represented the righteous remnant as well as the restored community. As the ancient Israelites had been, Jesus too was driven into the wilderness to be tested (Matthew 4; Mark 1; Luke 4). As the Israelites had wandered forty years in the wilderness, so Jesus lived forty days in the wilderness. Just as the Israelites had been tested three times (longing for bread, worshiping the gold calf idol, and complaining against God at Marah), so Jesus was also tested in these three areas during his wilderness experience. However, while the ancient Israelites failed their tests, Jesus completed his and fulfilled both the Scriptures and the divinely assigned role of Israel to be a light to the nations.

Third, *the gospels describe Jesus as a divine emperor who came back to* free *a people from captivity*. References to Jesus as Lord, Savior, and Messiah were direct attacks to the Roman Caesar. In Mark's gospel Jesus gathered large crowds, confronted the religious leaders in Judea, and quickly moved throughout the countryside gathering disciples, healing the sick, and performing miracles. In Luke's gospel Jesus led the masses of oppressed, suffering, and marginalized people to form an army seeking salvation and healing among the broader Jewish population. In John's gospel, Jesus was God, who received divine testimony through his miracles, through voices from heaven, and through the Torah. Jesus even confronted the Roman ruler Pilate by testifying to his own empire: "Jesus said, 'My kingdom is not of this world. If it were, my servants would fight to prevent my arrest by the Jewish leaders. But now my kingdom is from another place'" (John 18:36).

Matthew suggested that Jesus was the new Moses, the leader of the new Israel. Matthew's gospel includes five teaching blocks, which recall the five books of the Torah, and illustrate that Jesus's ministry focused on teaching and discipleship.[1] Matthew also describes Jesus as the one who, like Moses, ascended the mountain. But Jesus, unlike Moses, sat down on the mountain and invited his disciples to join him there (Matt 5:1). The Sermon on the Mount became a new Torah, one driven by compassion and social justice. Just as Yahweh had told the people in Jerusalem to

---

1. The five sections of Matthew each includes narrative (1–4; 8–9; 11:2—12:50; 13:54—17:27; 19:2—22:46), teaching (5–7; 10; 13; 18; 23–25), and a concluding statement (7:28–29; 11:1; 13:53; 19:1; 26:1).

remember the Torah (Mal 4:4), so Matthew told his community of Jewish Christ followers that Jesus fulfilled the Torah (Matt 5:17–18). The notion that Jesus fulfills the Hebrew Scriptures does not mean that the prophets' writings found fulfillment only in him; it means that even though the prophets' messages had meanings for their own times, Jesus completed the prophecies again. Just as those returning from Babylon to Jerusalem under Persian rule had only Yahweh as king, so the community of Jesus (which, the New Testament suggests, saw itself as a renewed Israel) held only Jesus as priest and king.

Jesus's connection to Israel and the prophets was also illustrated by Matthew's account of Jesus's healing the crowds (12:15–21). Matthew quoted Isa 42:1–4, which had three renderings in the Jewish community of his day:

> "Here is my servant whom I have chosen." (Hebrew text of Isa 42:1)
>
> "Here is Jacob, my chosen servant." (Greek [Septuagint] text of Isa 42:1)
>
> "Here is my messiah, whom I have chosen." (Aramaic [Targum] text of Isa 42:1)

Prophecies were applied in different situations; however, messianic interpretations were used to support the mission of God's people. In the book of Acts, for instance, Luke placed a text from Isaiah in the mouth of Paul to suggest that the church was also a fulfillment of messianic expectation of God's people. "I have made you a light for the Gentiles that you may bring salvation to the ends of the earth" (Acts 13:47).

Among the first communities of Christ followers Jesus and what became the church were understood to be vehicles for the transformation and restoration of God's people. Jesus is the God of second chances, who reconciles, restores, and reunites the fallen or captive people of God. Jesus is the judge of the wicked as well as the one who pours out the spirit to unite people to God.

Finally, *Jesus painted visions and hope for an alternate reality of the kingdom.* He referred to the empire as being "from above" (John 3:3–5; 19:36). His parables of the empire of God were told to motivate, to inspire hope and healing. As a teacher, Jesus inspired others to see God's reign as one of peace and as something that was near.

Jesus Restores Relationship

Jesus came to save people. However, this salvation does not refer to a simple prayer or guarantee that we will one day go to heaven. Salvation involved restoration, reconciliation, and reunion with God. Jesus brought people into relationship with the Creator. Salvation suggests relationship and peace with God. The pouring out, baptism, and covering with the Spirit also symbolized human relationships with God through Jesus. Christians today must embrace Jesus as the God of second chances in both their own lives and the lives of others. "The Christian movement must be the living, breathing promise to society that it is possible to live out the values of Christ—that is, to be a radical, troubling alternative to the power imbalances in the empire. In a world of greed and consumerism, the church ought to be a community of generosity and selflessness. In a host empire that is committed to marginalizing the poor, resisting the place of women, causing suffering to the disenfranchised, the Christian community must be generous to a fault, pursuant of justice, flushed with mercy."[2]

First, *Jesus restores us to a relationship with God*. He is God who judges and pours out the Spirit for relationship and a new covenant. Salvation is more than waiting for the Judgment Day and our death. Salvation involves peace, safety, and connection with God, the Creator of the universe, today. Restoration also involves repentance, forgiveness, hope, and love. Jesus gives us hope now! Yet he also calls us to a decision, a relationship, to a life that is renewed and full of hope—one that can overcome our past. We can know Jesus, not just as the one who frees us from slavery, but as one who is the God of multiple chances.

Second, *restoration involves repentance and turning our hearts to God*. The gospels began with a call to repentance. Repentance is not an apology. Repentance centers on behavior modification and a change to life. The Greek word for *repentance* means "a change of mind"; however, the Hebrew word for this same concept means "a change of direction." While the Greek has a difficult time capturing the Hebrew word, the Apostle Paul used other Greek terms to capture this Hebrew concept. Christians must return to the true meaning of repentance as behavior modification rather than to just an apology. Repentance is ongoing and requires hard work. Repentance takes time. Repentance requires that we make amends to those we have hurt, and do the difficult work to change our behavior and live in harmony and peace with others. Forgiveness and

2. Frost, *Exiles*, 15–16.

PART FOUR   Calling for Hope

grace empower us to continue in our repentance with hope that transformation is possible because acceptance and love is extended. Jesus today calls people to repentance, which opens the door for the Lord to enter and help us to become disciples in our journey with Jesus.

Third, *restoration involves the Spirit and the return of prophecy.* Over the years the Christian community has struggled to understand the Spirit, prophecy, and tongues. However, the Hebrew prophets testified under the influence of the Spirit, sharing God's message with people. The power of the Spirit in the ministry of Jesus was manifested by Jesus's teaching, preaching, and boldness. In the early church tongues/languages were a vehicle that the Spirit used to carry the message of Jesus throughout the world. Those who are restored in their relationship with God receive the permission and power to witness concerning God's love and passion for people locally and globally. Those in relationship with God have the opportunity to teach and preach because they experience God's nature and love.

Finally, *restoration suggests that we join Jesus in this work*: "The difficulty for the church today is not in encouraging people to ask what Jesus would do but in getting them to break out of their domesticated and sanitized ideas about Jesus in order to answer that question."[3] Since Jesus was incarnational, we must follow that practice. The church today must move out of our buildings and meet people in their locations. Creating sacred and safe spaces in our communities calls for courage. Jesus represented both God and the people of Israel. The restored kingdom was a kingdom on the move that connected with others in the camps of exile, along the rivers in Babylon, and in the ruins of Jerusalem. Both Yahweh and the prophets lived among the suffering people and brought messages of hope and comfort.

Likewise God's people today must rise up as did the prophets of old and meet the exiles in their camps or in the ruins of their lives. Jesus the friend of sinners is the God of second and multiple chances. Our message should provide hope and call for relationship with a God of passion, comfort, and healing. Our message is not one that condemns but provides grace, mercy, and compassion.

---

3. Frost and Hirsch, *ReJesus*, 19–20.

Jesus, the God of Second Chances

Providing Hope in a World of Darkness

The church today has been called to fulfill the role of the prophets in the Hebrew Scriptures. Jesus is the God of second chances who calls us not only to follow him but to reorient our lives to reflect his nature. He was God in the flesh; therefore we should follow. The prophets represented people and Yahweh, so should we. The prophets were traumatized by what they saw and heard. So should we also be impacted by what we see and hear.

Being a minister is exciting and frustrating. I hug a lot of people and would like to choke a few, or scream, "What the heck is the matter with you?" I hug, and don't do the other; however, many of us have been frustrated to that point. Yet as God's servants, we don't act on those violent impulses. Sometimes I weep with the people I meet. Other times I just listen in shock. We, like the prophets, dwell with the exiles because they need to know that God is with them. We must carry the message of hope to those in exile, in captivity, in the ruins of their lives.

First, *the Apostle Paul used the word "reconciliation" often in the Christian Scriptures.* Jesus reconciled people back to God and each other (Eph 1:10; 2:11–13; Col 1:20). This reconciliation was a restoration of relationship (through the pouring out of the Spirit), which brought peace (*shalom*) between God and people and among people. Paul even referred to the ministry of himself and his colleagues as a ministry of reconciliation: "If anyone is in Christ, the new creation has come: the old has gone, the new is here! This is from God, who reconciled us through Christ and gave us the ministry of reconciliation: that God was reconciling the world in Christ, not counting people's sins against them, and has given us the message of reconciliation. We are therefore Christ's ambassadors, as though God were making an appeal through us. We implore you on Christ's behalf: Be reconciled to God" (2 Cor 5:16–20).

To have a ministry of reconciliation means that the church seeks to introduce others to God and help them in their journey to draw closer to Jesus.

> We have come to see that mission is not merely an activity of the church. Rather, mission is the result of God's initiative, rooted in God's purposes to restore and heal creation. "Mission" means "sending," and it is the central biblical theme describing the purpose of God's action in human history ... God's mission continued then in the sending of the Spirit to call forth and empower

the church as the witness to God's good news in Jesus Christ. It continues today in the worldwide witness of churches in every culture to the gospel of Jesus Christ, and it moves toward the promised consummation of God's salvation in the *eschaton*.[4]

The ministry of reconciliation means that the church, like the ancient prophets, engage their communities, become advocates for Jesus and others, and seek to establish and envision God's *shalom*.

Second, *the church has been called to stand for the rights of others.* Social justice will be a major focus of a church which is prophetic. The prophets of old became a voice for God and for the oppressed: "The prophets were the guardians of the covenantal relationship between God and his people. They were obsessed with the call to faithfulness to God. And they insisted that true faithfulness toward God could not be fulfilled through religious ritual, but only with a heart given over to him."[5] Those on the margins of society have little voice in the community. However, God expects prophets to be that voice for the exiles, the remnant, and the oppressed. The church of second chances creates sacred and safe spaces for those oppressed in our society. We do this because as we are sent to people we find that their struggles are important to God. We are not only creating a new empire; we are empowering others to exist in a fading world. As prophets we must stand against injustice and advocate for both God and people: "By living incarnationally we not only model the pattern of humanity set up in the Incarnation but also create space for mission to take place in organic ways. In this way mission becomes something that 'fits' seamlessly into the ordinary rhythms of life, friendships, and community and is thus thoroughly contextualized."[6]

Christian people sometimes suggest that ministers should not be in the community. Maybe it is because they do not wish to be there themselves. However, to be a friend of sinners and tax collectors means that we are connected to people. We live in community and reach out to others at work, at our children's sporting events (we of all people should coach them and model love and compassion), in our neighborhoods, through our activities and service to our city. Through this we bring hope, love, mercy, repentance, and forgiveness to the community table of fellowship. They should know that prophets have been present.

---

4. Guder, *The Missional Church*, 4.
5. Frost and Hirsch, *ReJesus*, 71.
6. Hirsch, *The Forgotten Ways*, 135.

Finally, *we offer visions of hope in a new reality.* In 1 Corinthians the Apostle Paul shared that the system or empire was fading (1:28; 4:5; 7:31; 10:11; 13:8).[7] The permanent empire was the empire of *agape* love (1 Corinthians 13). *Agape* love is mature and develops a community to thrive in a temporary world/system. The church of second chances must be grounded in unconditional love and must offer this vision and hope for others. The empire of Jesus promotes peace, safety, acceptance, and support.

Ministry and Prophecy

I cannot count the number of times I have sat across from a young person, viewing them from the other side of protective glass or a cage, and talking through a prison telephone. It is sad to me. Young people who have made bad choices and face a potentially life-threatening existence in a place prison chaplains tell me is as close to hell as anyone will ever be. Prison is a nightmare for most that live there. Even more, it is a nightmare to these kids who never seemed to have a chance.

I have seen kids who have experienced abuse as children and grew to become dependent on alcohol, drugs, and sex to kill the pain and feelings of rejection. Their problem behavior escalates until they make the ultimate wrong choice and commit murder. One robbed an older man and then panicked and stabbed the man to death, even trying to sever his spinal cord. The prison guard who took me to meet this young man broke down crying when telling me about the boy's future in the prison system. I remember the young boy who robbed a convenience store (thank God he didn't shoot anyone) because it was "fun." I had baptized his brother and knew their family for years. He never had a fighting chance to make a better life for himself.

I can see in my mind the young women caught in prostitution who became so addicted to drugs that they lost their children and served time for their pimps. I remember the boys and girls locked in juvenile detention because they got into a fight; next, anger took over and they went too far. Even more I remember wrestling to find words of hope in a dark prison, an evil detention center, and a place filled with pain, suffering, and humiliation. What could I say to these young people? Did any of my words actually sound sincere, or were they just words of a middle class white guy who would leave and live in his nice, comfortable home?

7. Clark, *The Better Way*, 119–24.

PART FOUR   Calling for Hope

It really didn't matter. It's what you do when you are a minister. When people in their darkest hour cry out for help, you go—not because you are forced, but because someone has to reach them. You go because Jesus went, the apostles went, and Christians for two thousand years have gone.

The church of second chances joins others in exile and on the margins of society to provide hope and offer a vision of justice for themselves and their communities. This permeates our ministries not just in our Sunday morning worship but in our community service, discipleship, small groups, homes, families, and leadership. We model this vision when we create safe, sacred, and peaceful places. We model this vision as we create openness, trust, and honesty. Jesus and his servants called this *shalom*.

The church of second chances has tremendous opportunity not only to reach people but to offer them hope, an alternative reality, and peace. Introducing others to the God of second chances also fosters relationship between Creator and creation. The church that lives this way, like Ezekiel, proves to others that a prophet has been among them.

It's easy to tell people the way.

It's harder to show people the way.

It's even more difficult to walk with people along the way.

However, walking with others is truly what it means to be prophetic.

Bibliography

Ames, Frank Ritchel. "The Cascading Effects of Exile: From Diminished Resources to New Identity." In *Interpreting Exile: Displacement and Deportation in Biblical and Modern Contexts*, edited by Brad E. Kelle et al., 173–87. Society of Biblical Literature: Ancient Israel and Its Literature 10. Atlanta: Society of Biblical Literature, 2011.

Arnold, Bill T. "What Has Nebuchadnezzar to Do with David? On the Neo-Babylonian Period and Early Israel." In *Mesopotamia and the Bible: Comparative Explorations*, edited by Mark W. Chavalas and K. Lawson Younger Jr., 330–55. Grand Rapids: Baker Academic, 2002.

Balentine, Samuel E. "The Prose and Poetry of Exile." In *Interpreting Exile: Displacement and Deportation in Biblical and Modern Contexts*, edited by Brad E. Kelle et al., 345–63. Atlanta: Society of Biblical Literature, 2011.

Barton, John. *Joel and Obadiah*. Old Testament Library. Louisville: Westminster John/Knox, 2001.

Ben Zvi, Ehud. "Introduction: Writings, Speeches, and the Prophetic Books—Setting an Agenda." In *Writings and Speech in Israelite and Ancient Near Eastern Prophecy*, edited by Ehud Ben Zvi and Michael H. Floyd, 1–29. Society of Biblical Literature Symposium Series 10. Atlanta: Society of Biblical Literature, 2000.

Bleibtreu, Erika. "Grisly Assyrian Record of Torture and Death." *Biblical Archaeology Review* 17 (1991) 52–61, 75.

Bouma-Prediger, Steven, and Brian J. Walsh. *Beyond Homelessness: Christian Faith in a Culture of Displacement*. Grand Rapids: Eerdmans, 2008.

Brueggemann, Walter. *Cadences of Home: Preaching among Exiles*. Louisville: Westminster John Knox, 1997.

———. *Hopeful Imagination: Prophetic Voices in Exile*. Philadelphia: Fortress, 1986.

Childs, Brevard S. *Old Testament Theology in a Canonical Context*. Philadelphia: Fortress, 1985.

Clark, Ron. *Am I Sleeping with the Enemy? Males and Females in the Image of God*. Eugene, OR: Cascade Books, 2010.

———. *The Better Way: The Church of Agape in Emerging Corinth*. Eugene, OR: Pickwick Publications, 2010.

———. *Setting the Captives Free: A Christian Theology for Domestic Violence*. Eugene, OR: Cascade Books, 2005.

———. "Open Your Eyes." *Journal of Religion and Abuse* 4/1 (2002) 27–36.

PART ONE   Introduction: The God of Hope

Cooke, G. A. *A Critical and Exegetical Commentary on the Book of Ezekiel*. International Critical Commentary. Edinburgh: T. & T. Clark, 1985.

Crenshaw, James L. *Prophets, Sages, & Poets*. St. Louis: Chalice, 2006.

Denfeld, Rene. *All God's Children: Inside the Dark and Violent World of Street Families*. New York: PublicAffairs, 2007.

Dempsey, Carol. *The Prophets: A Liberation-Critical Reading*. A Liberation-Critical Reading of the Old Testament. Minneapolis: Fortress, 2000.

Epictetus. *Enchiridion*. Translated by George Long. Great Books in Philosophy. New York: Prometheus, 1991.

Eszenyei Széles, María. *Wrath and Mercy: A Commentary on the Books of Habakkuk and Zephaniah*. Translated by George A. F. Knight. International Theological Commentary. Grand Rapids: Eerdmans, 1987.

Fretheim, Terence E. *Exodus*. Interpretation. Louisville: Westminster John Knox, 1991.

Frost, Michael. *Exiles: Living Missionally in a Post-Christian Culture*. Peabody, MA: Hendrickson, 2006.

Frost, Michael, and Alan Hirsch. *ReJesus: A Wild Messiah for a Missional Church*. Peabody, MA: Hendrickson, 2009.

Garber David B., Jr. "A Vocabulary of Trauma in the Exilic Writings." In *Interpreting Exile: Displacement and Deportation in Biblical and Modern Contexts*, edited by Brad E. Kelle, et al., 309–22. Society of Biblical Literature: Ancient Israel and Its Literature 10. Atlanta: Society of Biblical Literature, 2011.

Grabbe, Lester L. "Ancient Near Eastern Prophecy from an Anthropological Perspective." In *Prophecy in Its Ancient Near Eastern Context: Mesopotamian, Biblical, and Arabian Perspectives*, edited by Martti Nissinen, 13–32. Society of Biblical Literature Symposium Series 13. Atlanta: Society of Biblical Literature, 2000.

Greenberg, Moshe. *Ezekiel 21–48*. Anchor Bible. Garden City, NY: Doubleday, 1997.

Gowan, Donald E. *Theology of the Prophetic Books: The Death and Resurrection of Israel*. Louisville: Westminster John Knox, 1998.

Guder, Darrell L., editor. *The Missional Church: A Vision for the Sending of the Church in North America*. Grand Rapids: Eerdmans, 1998.

Hiebert, Theodore. *The God of My Victory: The Ancient Hymn in Habakkuk 3*. Harvard Semitic Monographs 38. Atlanta: Scholars, 1998.

Hildebrandt, Ted. "Proverbs 22:6a: Train up a Child?" *Grace Theological Journal* 9/1 (1988) 3–19.

Hirsch, Alan. *The Forgotten Ways: Reactivating the Missional Church*. Grand Rapids: Brazos, 2006.

Holladay, William. *Jeremiah 1: A Commentary on the Book of the Prophet Jeremiah, Chapters 1–25*. Hermeneia. Philadelphia: Fortress, 1986.

Holton, M. Jan. "Imagining Hope and Redemption: A Salvation Narrative among the Displaced in Sudan." In *Interpreting Exile: Displacement and Deportation in Biblical and Modern Contexts*, edited by Brad E. Kelle et al., 217–33. Society of Biblical Literature: Ancient Israel and Its Literature 10. Atlanta: Society of Biblical Literature, 2011.

Howard-Brook, Wes. *"Come Out, My People!": God's Call out of Empire in the Bible and Beyond*. Maryknoll, NY: Orbis, 2010.

Irvine, Stuart A. *Isaiah, Ahaz, and the Syro-Ephraimitic Crisis*. Society of Biblical Literature Dissertation Series 123. Atlanta: Scholars, 1990.

Bibliography

Klein, Ralph W. *Israel in Exile: A Theological Interpretation*. Overtures to Biblical Theology 6. Philadelphia: Fortress, 1979.

Longman, Tremper, III. *How to Read Exodus*. Downers Grove, IL: IVP Academic, 2009.

Lorein, Geert W. "The Holy Spirit at Qumran." In *Presence, Power, and Promise: The Role of the Spirit of God in the Old Testament*, edited by David G. Firth and Paul D. Wegner, 371–95. Downers Grove, IL: InterVarsity, 2011.

MacDonald, John. "The Status and Role of the Na'ar in Israelite Society." *Journal of Near Eastern Studies* 35 (1976) 147–70.

Mandolfo, Carleen R. *Daughter Zion Talks Back to the Prophets: A Dialogic Theology of the Book of Lamentations*. Semeia Studies 58. Atlanta: Society of Biblical Literature, 2007.

Matthews, Victor H. *The Social World of the Hebrew Prophets*. Peabody, MA: Hendrickson, 2001.

McConville, J. G. *Judgment and Promise: An Interpretation of the Book of Jeremiah*. Leicester, UK: Apollos, 1993.

Meier, Samuel A. *Themes and Transformations in Old Testament Prophecy*. Downers Grove, IL: IVP Academic, 2009.

Mitchell, Don. *The Right to the City: Social Justice and the Fight for Public Space*. New York: Guilford, 2003.

Ntamushabora, Faustin. *From Trials to Triumphs: The Voice of Habakkuk for the Suffering African Christian*. Eugene, OR: Wipf & Stock, 2009.

Nemet-Nejat, Karen Rhea. *Daily Life in Ancient Mesopotamia*. Peabody, MA: Hendrickson, 2002.

Neusner, Jacob. *Transformations in Ancient Judaism: Textual Evidence for Creative Responses to Crisis*. Peabody: Hendrickson, 2004.

Nissinen, Martti, with contributions by C. L. Seow and Robert K. Ritner. *Prophets and Prophecy in the Ancient Near East*. Edited by Peter Machinist. Society of Biblical Literature Writings from the Ancient World 12. Atlanta: Society of Biblical Literature, 2003.

O'Connor, Kathleen M. "The Tears of God and Divine Character in Jeremiah 2–9." In *Troubling Jeremiah*, edited by A. R. Pete Diamond et al., 387–401. Journal for the Study of the Old Testament Supplement Series 260. Sheffield: Sheffield Academic, 1999.

Ortlund, Raymond C., Jr. *Whoredom: God's Unfaithful Wife in Biblical Theology*, New Studies in Biblical Theology. Grand Rapids: Eerdmans, 1996.

Petersen, David L. "Defining Prophecy and Prophetic Literature." In *Prophecy in Its Ancient Near Eastern Context: Mesopotamian, Biblical, and Arabian Perspectives*, edited by Martti Nissinen, 33–44. Society of Biblical Literature Symposium Series 13. Atlanta: Society of Biblical Literature, 2000.

———. *Late Israelite Prophecy: Studies in Deutero-Prophetic Literature and in Chronicles*. Society of Biblical Literature Monograph Series 23. Missoula: Scholars, 1977.

Plaut, W. Gunther. *The Book of Proverbs: A Commentary*. Jewish Commentary for Bible Readers. New York: Union of American Hebrew Congregations, 1961.

Redditt, Paul L. *Introduction to the Prophets*. Grand Rapids: Eerdmans, 2008.

Roberts, J. J. M. *Nahum, Habakkuk, and Zephaniah*. The Old Testament Library. Louisville: Westminster John Knox, 1991.

Smith, Mark S. *The Early History of God: Yahweh and the Other Deities in Ancient Israel*. 2nd ed. The Biblical Resource Series. Grand Rapids: Eerdmans, 2001.

PART ONE   Introduction: The God of Hope

———. *The Origins of Biblical Monotheism: Israel's Polytheistic Background and the Ugaritic Texts*. New York: Oxford University Press, 2001.

Smith-Christopher, Daniel L. *A Biblical Theology of Exile*. Overtures to Biblical Theology. Minneapolis: Fortress, 2002.

Stivers, Laura. *Disrupting Homelessness: Alternative Christian Approaches*. Prisms. Minneapolis: Fortress, 2011.

Thompson, J. A. *The Book of Jeremiah*. New International Commentary on the Old Testament. Grand Rapids: Eerdmans, 1980.

Thomas, R. Murray. *Moral Development Theories—Secular and Religious: A Comparative Study*. Contributions to the Study of Education 68. Westport, CT: Greenwood, 1997.

Tisdale, Leonora Tubbs. *Prophetic Preaching: A Pastoral Approach*. Louisville: Westminster John Knox, 2010.

Weems, Renita J. *Battered Love: Marriage, Sex, and Violence in the Hebrew Prophets*. Overtures to Biblical Theology. Minneapolis: Fortress, 1995.

Wiseman, D. J. *Nebuchadrezzar and Babylon*. Schweich Lectures 1983. Oxford: Oxford University Press, 1991.

Wolff, Hans Walter. *Joel and Amos*. Translated by Waldemar Janzen et al. Hermenia. Philadelphia: Fortress, 1977.

www.ingramcontent.com/pod-product-compliance
Lightning Source LLC
Chambersburg PA
CBHW020850160426
43192CB00007B/863